Man Up!

RANDALL J.
BREWER

MAN UP!

CONTENTS

INTRODUCTION

There is a quiet crisis unfolding in our world today not because men lack ability, intelligence, or potential, but because too many have surrendered their strength without even realizing it. Passivity has been sold as peace. Silence has been mislabeled as wisdom. Weakness has been wrapped in the language of humility. And somewhere along the way, many men have been convinced that standing down is more virtuous than standing up. This book exists to challenge that lie.

The term "Man Up!" is not a suggestion. It is not a slogan. It is not a motivational phrase meant to stir temporary emotion. It is a call - clear, direct, and uncompromising - to return to the kind of manhood that refuses to shrink, retreat, or remain silent in the face of responsibility. It is a summons to rise from the shadows of hesitation and reclaim the strength, courage, and boldness that were placed inside you by design.

Men were never created to drift through life on autopilot. They were formed to lead, to protect, to build, and to stand firm when pressure comes. Yet passivity has become the default posture of too many. It shows up in the unwillingness to make decisions, the fear of confrontation, the avoidance of responsibility, and the tendency to let life happen instead of shaping it. Passive men don't usually intend to be weak - they simply stop fighting for what matters.

This book is written for the man who knows, deep down, that there is more in him than what has been expressed so far. The man who senses a fire within but has allowed discouragement, fear, failure, or comfort to smother it. The man who is tired of sitting on the sidelines of his own life, watching opportunities pass, relationships suffer, and purpose remain unfulfilled. "Man Up!" is a declaration that passivity is no longer acceptable.

To "man up" does not mean becoming harsh, arrogant, or domineering. True strength is not loud insecurity, reckless aggression, or emotional detachment. Real manhood is marked by boldness with wisdom, confidence with humility, and strength that serves rather than hides. It is the ability to stand your ground without becoming cruel, to speak truth without fear, and to carry responsibility without complaint.

Strong men are not controlled by their emotions but neither do they run from them. Mighty men are not defined by the absence of fear but by the refusal to let fear dictate their actions. Bold men do not wait for permission to do what is right. They step forward when others step back.

This book confronts the modern narrative that men should apologize for being strong or feel guilty for taking the lead. It rejects the idea that masculinity is a problem to be managed rather than a gift to be stewarded. Strength is not toxic when it is disciplined. Authority is not dangerous when it is anchored in character. Confidence is not pride when it flows from purpose.

You were created to be strong and mighty not in your own ego, but in your convictions. You were designed to face adversity, to endure hardship, and to stand tall when pressure tries to bend you. History has never been shaped by passive men. Families are not built by indecision. Legacies are not formed by those who refuse to take responsibility.

This book will challenge you to examine where you have retreated instead of advanced. Where you have remained silent instead of speaking up. Where you have settled instead of rising. It will confront excuses, expose complacency, and dismantle the subtle habits that keep men stuck in neutral. But it will also equip you with clarity, direction, and the courage to move forward with strength.

"Man Up!" is about reclaiming the warrior's mindset - not one of violence, but of vigilance; not one of domination, but of determination. It is about learning to stand firm in conviction, to walk boldly in purpose, and to carry yourself as a man who knows who he is and why he is here.

The world does not need more passive men waiting to be told what to do. It needs men who are willing to step forward, take responsibility, and lead with courage. It needs men who refuse to quit, refuse to compromise their values, and refuse to live small when they were created for strength.

This is your call to reject passivity. This is your call to embrace boldness. This is your call to rise strong and stand mighty. This is your call to "Man Up!"

| 1 |

"GOD IS CALLING"

We are living in dark, difficult, and serious times and the men of God need to "Man Up!" In the beginning darkness was on the face of the deep and God said, "Let there be light" (Gen. 1:3). Today God wants you to "Man Up!" and be a light in this dark world (Matt. 5:14). When light fights against darkness, light always wins. On the Day of Pentecost, Acts 2:14 says, "But Peter, standing up with the eleven, raised his voice and said to the crowd..." In order to "Man Up!" you have to do 3 things. First, you have to be saved for there is no such thing as manhood without God, and there is no way to live it without being filled with the Holy Spirit. There is a lie circulating in our culture that manhood is something you can manufacture on your own through strength, success, discipline, or willpower. But Scripture tells a very different story. Man was never designed to be self-sufficient. From the beginning, God formed man from the dust and then breathed into him the breath of life.

Without that breath, Adam was only a body. He was present, but powerless. In the same way, a man today can have a body, a title, a career, even respect, yet still lack the life and strength God intended because he is empty of the Spirit. The Holy Spirit is not optional. He is not a religious accessory or an emotional experience. He is the power source of godly manhood. Without the Spirit, a man may be loud but not loving, strong but not steadfast, driven but not disciplined, bold but not holy. Flesh can imitate toughness, but only the Spirit produces self-control, humility, courage, and endurance. True manhood is not about domination - it is about dominion. Not over people, but over sin, fear, pride, and temptation. And that kind of dominion cannot be achieved through grit alone. Jesus Himself declared that the flesh profits nothing. Victory comes only when a man is led, strengthened, and governed by the Spirit of God.

A man filled with the Holy Spirit does not react - he responds. He does not crumble under pressure - he stands firm. He does not run from responsibility - he carries it with grace. He loves sacrificially, leads faithfully, and endures patiently not because he is strong in himself, but because God is strong in him. Manhood without God is empty masculinity. It is form without power, appearance without substance. But when a man is filled with the Holy Spirit, he becomes what God intended him to be - a man of conviction, compassion, courage, and character. So the call is clear: Be filled with the Spirit. Not once, not occasionally, but daily. Lay down self-reliance. Surrender pride. Make room for God's power. Because the greatest men are not those who trust in their own strength but those who allow the

Spirit of the living God to shape, lead, and empower every part of their lives. There is no true manhood without God. And there is no godly manhood without the Holy Spirit.

Next, you have to stand up for there is no such thing as complacent manhood. Manhood was never designed to be passive. There is no neutral gear in a man's life. You are either standing up or sliding back. You are either engaged or drifting. Complacency is not rest - it is retreat and retreat always comes at a cost. A man who refuses to stand will eventually fall - if not outwardly, then inwardly. God did not create men to watch life happen from the sidelines. He formed men to guard, build, lead, and protect. From the beginning, Adam was placed in the garden to tend it and keep it. That word "keep" means 'to guard, defend, and take responsibility.' Complacency was never part of the assignment. When a man grows comfortable, his convictions weaken. When his convictions weaken, compromise enters. And when compromise enters, strength quietly exits. What a man tolerates today will dominate him tomorrow. Every man is being shaped either by what he confronts or by what he allows.

Many men don't fall suddenly - they drift slowly. They tolerate unguarded thoughts, lingering bitterness, private habits, justified anger, spiritual laziness, and unchecked pride. At first, all these things feel manageable, harmless, and contained. But tolerance is never neutral. It is an agreement, and every agreement empowers what you permit. Scripture warns us clearly in Eph. 4:27, "Do not give place to the devil." The enemy doesn't need control - he only needs access. Sin never stays small. Compromise never stays contained. Unchecked thoughts never remain private. What you excuse today will enslave you tomorrow. That anger becomes rage. That lust becomes bondage. That fear becomes paralysis. That apathy becomes spiritual death. But the reverse is also true. Whatever a man feeds will grow. Whatever a man confronts will weaken. What you fight will die. What you resist today will retreat tomorrow. What you crucify today will lose power tomorrow. What you cut off today will not control you later.

A man of God does not negotiate with sin, and he does not coexist with compromise. He does not "manage" what God calls him to mortify. Jesus said it plainly, "If your right hand causes you to sin, cut it off" (Matt. 5:30). Not because God is harsh, but because sin is lethal. Strong men draw lines before the battle reaches their doorstep. Standing up does not always mean raising your voice - it means raising your standard. It means saying, "Not in my house. Not in my heart. Not on my watch." A complacent man avoids confrontation. A godly man confronts what threatens his purpose. Standing up means taking responsibility for your soul, your family, your integrity, and your walk with God. It means refusing to blame circumstances, people, or the past. Faith demands posture, truth demands action, and manhood demands courage. There is no such thing as a complacent man who finishes strong. This is the hour to stand up. Not tomorrow. Not when it's convenient. Now. Be like Peter. Stand up and "Man Up!"

Finally, you have to raise your voice for there is no such thing as silent manhood. A real man was never designed to be quiet. God did not create men to fade into the background, whisper convictions, or silently watch as truth is trampled and families, faith, and futures are threatened. From the beginning of time manhood carried a voice, a charge, and a responsibility. Yes, there are moments when silence is wisdom but a silent man in the face of wrong is not wise; it is foolishness. When Adam stood beside Eve in the garden, his greatest failure was not action - it was inaction. He was present, but he did not speak. He did not intervene. He did not raise his voice. And silence opened the door to the fall. Ever since then, silence has been one of the enemy's most effective weapons against men. If the enemy can keep a man quiet, he can keep him passive. If he can keep him passive, he can keep him powerless. This is why a man must stand up and raise his voice.

To raise your voice does not mean to be loud, angry, or abusive. It means to be clear, firm, and unashamed. A man raises his voice when truth is being compromised, when his family is being threatened spiritually, when his integrity is being tested, when his children need direction, and when his faith demands obedience. Manhood speaks when it would be easier to stay quiet. A man who never raises his voice will never raise standards. A man who never speaks will never lead. God responds to men who speak, men who declare, command, and stand. Men cried out and God answered. Men confronted and God backed them. Men spoke boldly and heaven moved. God has never advanced His kingdom through timid silence. He moves through men who open their mouths and align their words with His will. Your voice matters because authority is released through speech. Faith speaks. Courage speaks. Conviction speaks. Silence never drove out darkness - light does, and light must be declared.

The truth be told, quiet men create loud problems. When men refuse to speak confusion grows, evil advances, families drift, and culture decays. What you tolerate in silence, you eventually suffer in reality. Manhood is not proven by how much you endure quietly, but by how boldly you stand when it counts. Now is the time to be heard. God is not begging men to speak - He is calling them. Now is the time to raise your voice in prayer, raise your voice in truth, raise your voice in leadership, and raise your voice in love and righteousness. This generation does not need quieter men - it needs clearer ones. Men who know what they believe, why they believe it, and are unafraid to say it. Remember, there is no such thing as silent manhood. A man who will not speak will never fully become who God called him to be. A man who refuses to speak forfeits part of his calling not because God withdraws it, but because the man refuses to walk into it. Now is the time to speak. Now is the time to raise your voice.

We live in a culture that coddles weakness and excuses passivity, especially in men. Responsibility is avoided. Commitment is postponed. Leadership is outsourced. But God has never lowered His standard to match culture. God is not standing in heaven wringing His hands, hoping someone will step up. God is calling all men to man up and be the man He created them to be. He is calling - not begging. Paul does not whisper to men; he commands them in 1 Cor. 16:13, "Be watchful. Stand firm. Act like men. Be strong." That phrase "be brave" literally means to "act like men." This is not arrogance. This is not dominance. This is biblical manhood. This language assumes resistance, pressure, and danger. Biblical manhood is forged in tension, not comfort. God is not pleading for volunteers - He is issuing orders to sons. The call of God has always been clear, strong, and decisive. From Genesis to Revelation, God calls men to stand, lead, obey, and walk in courage.

Many men today confuse grace with passivity. But grace does not remove responsibility; it restores it. God's grace calls men out of hiding, out of silence, and out of spiritual laziness. Adam fell not because he was weak physically, but because he was passive spiritually. When he hid among the trees, God did not ask out of ignorance, "Where are you?" He asked to summon a man back into responsibility. Grace has always done this. Grace does not excuse hiding; it exposes it so healing and restoration can begin. Hiding can look spiritual - busy church attendance, good behavior, quiet compliance - but it is still hiding. Men hide behind fear, shame, failure, and disappointment. They hide behind work, hobbies, addictions, and even religion. But grace steps into the shadows and says, "Come out. You were not created to live unseen." Grace calls all men out of silence. It does not shame a man for where he is - it invites him into who he was meant to be.

Silence is not humility when God has called you to speak. Too many men know the truth but refuse to declare it. They see injustice and stay quiet. They sense God's stirring and say nothing. They allow passivity to wear the mask of peace. Grace calls men out of spiritual laziness. It gives men a voice again. It teaches them to pray aloud, to speak truth with courage, to lead their homes, and to stand for righteousness without apology. Grace does not make men timid - it makes them bold and accountable. Grace is not permission to coast. It is power to rise up and take the world by storm. Spiritual laziness settles for minimal effort, shallow prayer, and borrowed convictions. It waits to be fed instead of learning to seek. It wants blessing without discipline and victory without battle. But grace trains us. Grace strengthens us. The same grace that saves a man also summons him to maturity. It calls him to wake up, to put on spiritual armor, to run his race with endurance, and to finish strong.

Grace is not begging men to follow God - it is calling them to stand up. This is the hour for men to rise, not in their own strength, but empowered by the grace of God that restores, equips, and sends. This is not the hour for retreat. This is not the hour for silence, excuses, or passivity. This is the hour for men to rise, not in the strength of muscle, not in the confidence of personality, and not in the pride of self-will. This is the hour for men to rise by the grace of God. God has never called men to save themselves. He calls men to be restored, equipped, and sent by His power and not their own. Grace does not weaken a man; it remakes him. Grace does not excuse failure; it redeems it. Grace does not leave a man where it finds him; it raises him to where God intended him to stand. Many men have been wounded in life, but the grace of God restores what was broken, revives what was buried, and reclaims what the enemy said was lost. This is the hour for restored men to rise.

God's grace not only heals but it also equips. Grace teaches a man how to stand when the pressure is heavy. Grace strengthens him to lead when it would be easier to withdraw. Grace forms courage, humility, discipline, and endurance in the inner man. The world does not need louder men. It needs men who are strong in character, strong in conviction, strong in love, strong in faith. And when God restores and equips a man, He does not leave him idle. He sends men back into their homes as leaders who love and serve. He sends men into their churches as pillars, not spectators. He sends men into their communities as examples of righteousness, integrity, and compassion. He sends men into battle not with fists raised in anger, but with hearts anchored in truth and lives surrendered to God. This is not a call to domination; this is a call to responsibility. This is not a call to pride; this is a call to purpose. Let restored men rise. Let equipped men stand. Let sent men go. Men of God, this is your hour.

We are not living in a crisis of masculinity because men are too strong. We are living in a crisis because too many men have become comfortable where God called them to be courageous. This generation celebrates ease, avoids discomfort, and mistakes passivity for peace. But Scripture never defined strength as loud aggression or brute force. True strength is the ability to stand, endure, repent, lead, and change when everything in you wants to stay the same. Soft men are not gentle men, they are men who refuse responsibility. A soft man avoids conviction; a strong man responds to it. A soft man blames his past; a strong man learns from it. A soft man protects his pride; a strong man crucifies it. Softness is not sensitivity; it is surrender to comfort. There is nothing godly about being weak in discipline, weak in prayer, weak in truth, and weak in resolve. God never called men to be numb, passive, or spiritually asleep. He called men to watch, stand firm, act like men, and be strong - not in ego, but in obedience.

Soft men fear confrontation. Soft men fear accountability. Soft men fear the pain of change more than the pain of staying broken. It takes strength to change. Strength is not the absence of fear - it is the decision to obey God despite it. Anyone can stay the same. Anyone can make excuses. Anyone can point fingers. But it takes a strong man to say, "I was wrong. I need help. I will change. I will submit to God." Change requires humility, and humility is not weakness - it is power under control. The strongest men in Scripture were not flawless men. They were men who responded to God's correction. When confronted, they repented. When corrected, they adjusted. When called, they moved. God is not asking men to become softer. He is calling them to become stronger in spirit, sharper in conviction, and deeper in character. Strong men pray when it's inconvenient, lead when it's uncomfortable, stand when it's unpopular, change when it's painful. They understand that discipline precedes freedom, and obedience precedes power.

The world doesn't need softer men - it needs transformed men. Families don't need passive men, churches don't need silent men, communities don't need distracted men. They need men who are strong enough to change, brave enough to repent, disciplined enough to grow, and humble enough to be led by God. This is not a call to arrogance. This is a call to have spiritual backbone. This is a call to man up! If you feel convicted, that is not condemnation - it is an invitation to become the man God created you to be. God does not expose weakness to shame you; He exposes it to strengthen you. The crisis of soft men will only be solved when men decide that comfort is no longer acceptable and obedience is non-negotiable. God is calling all men to be strong enough to change, humble enough to grow, and disciplined enough to lead. God is calling men not to be soft, but to walk in holiness and be strong in spirit, to lead with integrity, to live disciplined lives, to be firm in truth and faithful in action.

The questions to be asked are, "Who are you? What defines you? What makes you a man?" You're not defined by what you do for God; you're defined by what He already did for you. Gal. 2:20, "I have been crucified with Christ; it is no longer I who live, but Christ lives in me." You can't "Man Up!" until you know who you are in Christ.1 Cor. 15:10 says, "By the grace of God I am what I am." Who are you? You are the light of the world, a city on a hill. You are salt and light - men of the Word. You are prophetic and not pathetic. You are disciples. witnesses, Christ-followers. You are apostles, prophets, evangelists, pastors, and teachers. You are children of the cross, fruit of the empty tomb, a product of the upper room. You are the redeemed of the Lord, the sheep of His pasture. You are forgiven, free, and favored. You are called and chosen. You are warriors and worshipers. You are world-changers and history-makers. You are a man of God! Stand up and "Man Up!"

| 2 |

"BOYS NO MORE"

There is a tragic epidemic in the body of Christ today - not a lack of converts, not a lack of churches, not even a lack of knowledge - but a lack of men with spiritual maturity. They say they believe but lack the backbone to prove it. They love the milk of the Word but resist the meat of the Word. They want comfort but avoid responsibility. They have no problem asking God to do something but like Jonah they run away when God asks them to do something. Paul said plainly, "When I was a child, I spoke as a child, I understood as a child, I thought as a child; but when I became a man, I put away childish things" (1 Cor. 13:11). God is calling all men to go from boyhood to backbone, from spiritual adolescence to spiritual adulthood. He wants men to be boys no more. He wants them to grow up, and He wants them to man up! There is nothing wrong with being a child unless you are supposed to be a man. Childhood is not a sin, and immaturity is not a crime unless it becomes a refuge from responsibility.

The tragedy is not that a man was once a child, the tragedy is when a man stays a child, when a man refuses to grow up. The Apostle Paul is not condemning childhood; he is celebrating growth. Childhood is a season. It has a purpose. But it is never meant to be permanent. God expects His children to grow - not just in age, but in understanding, responsibility, and spiritual depth. Paul said at one time he spoke as a child. Childish speech is reactive, emotional, careless, and often self-centered. It speaks before it listens. It tears down instead of building up. It complains instead of trusting. Spiritual maturity changes how you talk. A mature believer speaks with grace, wisdom, restraint, and truth. Words are no longer weapons or emotional outlets but become instruments of life. When you grow up in Christ, you learn that your words carry weight, and you choose them carefully. Spiritual adulthood doesn't silence you; it disciplines you to say the right things at the right time, and to be silent when appropriate to do so.

Early in his life Paul had childish understanding. He understood as a child who sees only the moment, a child who lives by feelings, a child who expects life to be fair and easy. But spiritual maturity understands process. It understands that God works through seasons, pressure, delay, and discipline. A mature man no longer asks, "Why is this happening to me?" but instead asks, "What is God producing in me?" Understanding grows when faith is tested. Immaturity resists correction but maturity welcomes it. Faith that is never tested remains shallow. It may be sincere, but it is unproven. Scripture shows us that understanding is not gained in comfort but is forged in trial. When faith is challenged, stretched, and even shaken, something deeper begins to form within us. We move beyond what we heard into what we know. Testing exposes where our faith truly rests. When everything is easy, belief costs little. But when pressure comes, faith is invited to grow up. That is where understanding is born.

Immaturity resists correction. It wants affirmation without transformation and comfort without change. Maturity, however, welcomes correction. A mature man of God understands that loving correction is not rejection - it is an investment. God corrects those He is shaping, not those He is discarding. When faith is tested, maturity leans in instead of pulling away. It listens, learns, and allows God to refine motives, attitudes, and assumptions. Testing does not weaken true faith - it clarifies it. Through correction, God removes what is childish so that what is Christlike can remain. Understanding grows when you stop fighting the process and start trusting the Instructor. The same trial that frustrates the immature becomes a classroom for the mature. Spiritual growth is not proven by how loudly you profess faith, but by how humbly you receive instruction. When faith is tested and correction is embraced, wisdom takes root. And with wisdom comes stability, discernment, and depth.

Added to Paul's one-time childish behavior was the fact that he thought as a child. Childish thinking is centered on self, on one's comfort, their rights, and their personal preferences. It avoids responsibility and resents accountability. But when a man matures in Christ, his thinking shifts. He thinks long-term and becomes kingdom-minded and others-focused. He understands that freedom comes with responsibility, and blessing comes with stewardship. Mature thinking means you will no longer be led by impulse, fear, or offense. Immaturity is comfortable but very costly. Remaining childish feels safe because it avoids pressure, accountability, and sacrifice. But comfort always comes at a price. Families suffer, marriages weaken, and leadership disappears. Boys grow up without examples and society collapses from the absence of backbone. God never called men to live protected lives - He called them to live purposeful lives.

This is why Paul came to a point in his life where he put away childish things. Notice that no one did it for him. He took responsibility for his growth. Spiritual maturity is a decision. It is choosing to let go of excuses, emotional instability, offense, passivity, and spiritual laziness. Putting away childish things often feels uncomfortable because growth always costs something. But what you lay down in immaturity, you pick up in strength, clarity, and authority. God is not looking for perfect people - He is looking for mature believers who can be trusted with influence, responsibility, and purpose. This is not a call to abandon joy, wonder, or humility. It is a call to abandon immaturity and step into spiritual manhood - to stand firm, speak wisely, think clearly, and live intentionally. It is a call to man up! Childhood is a gift; maturity is a responsibility. What begins as dependence must grow into stewardship. The question is not whether you were once a child. The question is whether you are willing to grow.

Manhood is a calling from on high and not an age. Turning eighteen does not make a man. Growing a beard does not make a man. Strength, income, or titles do not make a man. A man is someone who accepts responsibility, keeps his word, protects what God entrusts to him, disciplines his desires, and stands when others shrink back. Manhood is not toxic, but passivity is. This is why the enemy loves childish men. Satan doesn't fear strong men - he fears grown men of God. A childish man is easy to distract. avoids confrontation, lives for pleasure, and always blames others. But a mature man prays when it's hard. He stays when it's uncomfortable. He leads when it's lonely. He obeys God when it costs him something. Grow up - not for your ego, but for your assignment. The world does not need more boys in grown bodies. It needs men with backbone, humility, and faith. Now is the time to grow up - not out of pressure, but out of purpose.

Spiritual maturity is not about knowing more scriptures - it's about growing up and becoming more dependable. Consider Jesus who was the perfect picture of a man with backbone. He did not remain in the manger. He grew. He submitted. He worked. He obeyed. He laid down His life. That is manhood. Jesus did not fold under pressure. He stood silent before accusers, He stayed obedient unto death, He carried the cross without compromise. He modeled spiritual maturity in His submission to the Father, in His courage in suffering, in His strength under restraint. If Christ endured the cross, surely you can endure the process. Scripture makes it very clear that there is a time when God expects growth. We live in a generation where immaturity is excused, celebrated, and even defended. Responsibility is avoided. Accountability is rejected. And growing up is treated like oppression. But God does not bless stagnation. Paul does not apologize for childhood. He testifies that growth and maturity is required.

God is a God of order. He designed growth to be progressive. There is a season to be taught, a season to be trained, a season to be trusted. No farmer plants seed expecting it to remain seed forever. Anything that refuses to grow is eventually removed. Understand that child-likeness is biblical, childishness is not. We must distinguish between two things scripture never confuses. Child-likeness depends on the Father and believes without skepticism and doubt. Jesus praised this type of behavior. Childishness, on the other hand, avoids responsibility, resists discipline, demands comfort, and blames others. Scripture rebukes this. 1 Cor. 14:20 says, "Brothers, do not be children in your thinking but be mature in understanding." In other words, child-likeness draws you toward God while childishness keeps you from becoming who God called you to be. You must always be aware that immaturity feels safe but it is very expensive. Immaturity promises comfort but produces consequences.

When men refuse to grow up, homes suffer, wives carry unnecessary weight, children grow up without examples, churches lack leaders, and society weakens. Heb. 5:12 says, "For though by this time you ought to be teachers, you need someone to teach you again the basic principles. You need milk, not solid food." Notice the phrase "by this time." The writer of Hebrews looks at believers who have spent time in the faith and says, "You should be further along now." Time passed. Opportunity was given. But growth did not happen. This verse is not a condemnation - it is a diagnosis. He's saying God expects progress that corresponds with time invested. You can sit in church for years and still be spiritually undeveloped. You can hear sermons weekly and never apply them daily. You can know scripture about God without knowing God deeply. Spiritual maturity is not automatic - it is intentional. Just as a child does not grow strong by birthday candles alone, a believer does not grow strong by calendar years alone.

The truth be told, milk is good until it's all you ever want. Milk represents basic truths, things such as salvation, forgiveness, God's love, grace, and mercy. These are essential foundations of the Christian faith, but they were never meant to be the finish line. Milk is for infants; meat is for the mature. When a believer refuses solid food, it often shows up as an inability to handle correction, to have a shallow understanding of scripture, emotional reactions instead of spiritual discernment, and dependence on others for every spiritual insight. God never intended His people to live on spiritual bottle-feeding forever. Maturity, on the other hand, is marked by responsibility. The writer says by now "you ought to be teachers." This does not mean everyone must preach but everyone should be able to share, model, and explain truth. Spiritual maturity shows up when you can encourage others with scripture, you can discern right from wrong, you can stand firm under pressure, you can feed yourself spiritually instead of waiting to be spoon-fed.

Later in Hebrews 5, we are told that solid food is for those who have trained their senses by practice. Maturity is developed, not downloaded. We live in a world where almost everything is instant. With a few taps, we can download information, order food, and access answers in seconds. But spiritual maturity does not work that way. You cannot download faithfulness. You cannot install endurance. You cannot stream wisdom. Spiritual maturity is formed the old-fashioned way - through time, testing, obedience, and perseverance. The writer of Hebrews reminds us that maturity comes by use, by practice and repetition. Milk is for the inexperienced, but solid food belongs to those who have exercised their spiritual senses. Growth happens when truth is lived, not just learned. Many believers want the results of maturity without the process. They want strength without resistance, victory without discipline, and depth without devotion. They don't realize that God develops maturity through seasons, not shortcuts.

Just as muscles grow under resistance, spiritual maturity is built through trials. Challenges are not signs of God's absence; they are often tools of His development. What you walk through today is training you for what you will stand in tomorrow. We live in a culture that assumes difficulty means something is wrong. People say, "If God were with me, this wouldn't be happening." Scripture, however, tells a very different story. Some of God's greatest work is done not in the removal of hardship, but in the use of it. What you are walking through today is not meant to break you - it is meant to build you up and make you strong. God does not waste seasons. He does not allow pain without purpose or pressure without design. Every challenge you face is shaping your character, sharpening your faith, and strengthening your spiritual muscles. Just as no soldier is trained in comfort and no athlete is developed without resistance, no believer is matured without testing. Trials are not punishments; they are preparations.

You may feel stretched, pressed, or overwhelmed, but stretching produces capacity. Pressure produces strength. Resistance produces endurance. God is developing in you what your future assignment will require. The weight you carry today is training you to stand under greater responsibility tomorrow. Joseph's pit prepared him for the palace. David's pasture prepared him for the throne. Jesus' time in the wilderness prepared Him for public ministry. What looks like delay is often development. What feels like opposition is often instruction. God is teaching you how to trust Him deeper, walk straighter, stand firmer, and endure longer than you ever could without the challenge. Do not despise the process. Do not resent the resistance. Do not misinterpret the trial as abandonment. God is strengthening your faith, refining your obedience, and aligning your heart with His purpose. When you stand in tomorrow's victory, you will look back and realize that today's struggle was not an obstacle - it was a training ground.

What you walk through today is preparing you for what you will stand in tomorrow. So stand firm, stay faithful, and keep walking because maturity is not proven by moments of inspiration but by daily consistency. Spiritual maturity is not revealed in a single emotional moment, a powerful altar call, or a surge of inspiration. Those moments can be meaningful, but they are not the measure of maturity. Maturity is proven in what you do consistently when no one is watching and nothing feels dramatic. Anyone can be inspired for a moment. It takes maturity to be faithful every day. The Christian life is not built on spiritual highs but on steady obedience. Inspiration may get you moving, but consistency is what carries you forward. Many believers love the feeling of being stirred, but far fewer are committed to the discipline of staying faithful when the feeling fades. Yet it is in those quiet, ordinary days that real growth happens. It's when you develop into authentic manhood, when you rise up and man up!

Jesus said, "If you love Me, keep My commandments" (John 14:15). Love is proven through obedience, and obedience is proven through consistency. Maturity shows up in prayer when you don't feel spiritual, in integrity when cutting corners would be easier, and in perseverance when quitting would be more comfortable. A child lives by impulse. A mature believer lives by principle. Children chase excitement; mature men and women embrace responsibility. Children wait to feel motivated; mature believers do what is right because it is right. Feelings fluctuate, but discipline remains. The Bible reminds us to "be steadfast, immovable, always abounding in the work of the Lord" (1 Cor. 15:58). Steadfastness does not mean spectacular - it means stable. It means showing up again tomorrow with the same commitment you had yesterday. God is far more impressed with a consistent walk than a dramatic moment. He is moved more by a faithful walk than by a momentary surge of passion.

God honors consistency over intensity. What truly pleases God is not a powerful moment but a faithful life that grows spiritually mature day by day. Spiritual maturity is forged in daily habits like opening the Word when no one is watching, spending time alone communing with God, praying when answers are not immediate, choosing obedience when temptation is knocking at your door, and serving when recognition is absent. These are not glamorous acts, but they are holy ones. God is not looking for occasional flashes of devotion; He is looking for faithful endurance. Inspiration may move your heart, but consistency shapes your character. Over time, consistent obedience produces spiritual strength, discernment, and authority. What feels small today becomes powerful tomorrow through repetition and faithfulness. Maturity understands that growth is a process. A tree does not grow overnight, yet day by day it puts down deeper roots. Storms do not destroy trees with deep roots - they reveal them.

In the same way, trials reveal who has been consistently grounded in God and who has only lived on moments of inspiration. True maturity understands that God honors perseverance. He rewards those who walk with Him daily, not just those who feel moved occasionally. So do not measure your spiritual life by how inspired you feel - measure it by how faithfully you live. Consistency is the quiet proof of maturity. And in the end, it is not the inspired moments that finish the race - it is the disciplined steps taken every single day. You can hear a thousand sermons and still remain immature if truth never moves from your head to your heart and into your hands. Maturity is truth applied, character tested, and faith proven. The Lord is calling His people to leave the nursery, take responsibility, and step into maturity. It's time to grow up in Christ, to move from being taught to teaching, from being fed to feeding, from surviving to strengthening others. The table is set. The meat is ready. The question is - are we willing to grow?

| 3 |

"HOLY DISCOMFORT"

G od's call to "Man up!" is not a motivational slogan, a cultural preference, or a polite invitation. It is a divine command spoken with authority, backed by heaven, and aimed straight at the heart of every man who claims to follow Him. When 1 Cor. 16:13 says, "Be watchful, stand firm in the faith, act like men, be strong, " God is not offering advice, He is issuing orders. Heaven does not negotiate maturity. God does not plead for obedience. He commands it. God didn't beg Noah to build the ark, He didn't plead with Abraham to leave Ur, He didn't negotiate with Moses at the burning bush, and He didn't soften the terms for Joshua at the Jordan. Joshua said to the people, "Choose for yourselves this day whom you will serve" (Josh. 24:15). Notice the word "choose." God honors free will, but He also demands decisiveness. Indecision is not humility, passivity is not patience, and delay is often disguised disobedience. A man of God must understand this truth: God calls men to respond, not to debate.

We are living in a time when strength is mocked, conviction is questioned, and manhood is being redefined by comfort instead of calling. But God has not changed His voice, and He has not softened His command. When God says, "Act like men," He is not offering encouragement. He is issuing a command. God does not beg men to mature; He does not negotiate obedience. He does, however, command responsibility. From the beginning, God placed responsibility on man. Adam was not asked if he felt ready to lead, guard, or obey - he was expected to do it. When Adam failed, God didn't ask Eve where Adam was. Why? Because leadership, accountability, and spiritual authority are not optional for men - they are assigned. To "man up" means to take responsibility instead of shifting blame, to stand firm instead of backing down, to lead with conviction instead of waiting for permission. Biblical manhood is forged in pressure, not passivity, obedience, not excuses, courage, not comfort.

Life is a battle so you must rise up and fight. Life is not a playground; it is a battlefield and only the strong survive. From the moment a man takes responsibility for his soul, his family, his calling, and his future, he steps into conflict. There is no neutral ground. There is no pause button. And there is no such thing as comfortable manhood. Comfort is the enemy of calling. Every man wants peace, but few want the price that peace requires. We want victory without struggle, strength without resistance, and crowns without crosses. But heaven has never promised comfort - it has promised purpose. And purpose is always forged in battle. A man becomes a man not by avoiding hardship, but by rising up to face it. Whether you like it or not, life will test you, your faith will be challenged, your integrity will be pressured, and your resolve will be attacked. The enemy doesn't take days off, and neither does responsibility. If you refuse to fight, you don't get peace - you get defeat.

There is no growth without resistance, no strength without strain, and no maturity without pain. Manhood is not built in comfort zones. It is forged in fire. Be aware that comfort produces cowards. Comfort whispers, "Take it easy," while God is calling you to stand up and fight like a man. Comfort teaches men to avoid risk, shrink responsibility, and numb conviction. It produces men who sit when they should stand, retreat when they should advance, and compromise when they should contend. Real men don't ask, "How can I stay comfortable?" They ask, "Where's the giant?" A man who seeks comfort will always sacrifice his destiny to protect his feelings, but a real man will fight for what matters. He'll fight for faith when doubt creeps in, for purity when temptation knocks, for discipline when laziness pulls, for his family when pressure rises, and for his calling when fear speaks. This fight is not optional - it is essential. Life rewards fighters, not spectators. Heaven honors men who refuse to quit.

You don't fight because you enjoy the battle. You fight because what's on the other side is worth it. This is not the time to sit back. This is not the season to play it safe. This is not the hour for soft living. Life is a battle and now is the time to rise up, take responsibility, stand your ground, and advance when others retreat. There is no such thing as comfortable manhood. There is only obedient, disciplined, battle-tested manhood so rise up and fight like the man you were created to be. Remove mediocrity, fear, apathy, complacency, and passivity from your life. Why? Because you are what you tolerate. Remove those obstacles that stop you from being a city on a hill. You are in a spiritual battle so rise up! Ps. 118:17 says, "I shall not die, but live, and declare the works of the Lord." Stand up and change the world for Jesus. Your mission in life is to help make the lives of other people better. You shine brightest not when you promote that which is perfect, but when you bless the broken.

You're here to be a light wherever you go so let your actions speak louder than your words. "Man Up!" and be the man God called you to be. The world teaches that strength is proven by dominance, by those who speaks loudest, stands tallest, or commands the most attention. But the kingdom of God turns that idea upside down. In God's economy, the strongest person in the room is often the one kneeling, lifting, washing, carrying, and serving. Jesus - who possessed all authority, all power, and all glory - chose the posture of a servant. He did not lead by intimidation but by incarnation. He stepped into the mess of humanity, bore burdens that were not His own, and lifted people who could never repay Him. This is the strength heaven celebrates. Real strength does not crush others to rise higher. Real strength does not demand recognition. Real strength uses its power to protect, encourage, and restore. Christlike leadership is not about being served, it is about choosing to serve.

Real men have the courage to lay ego aside, the discipline to show up when no one is watching, and the humility to value people more than position. Weakness avoids responsibility. Strength embraces it for the sake of others. When you serve, you are not diminishing yourself but are demonstrating maturity. When you lift others, you reflect the heart of Christ. This is the kind of strength that builds families, heals communities, and advances God's kingdom. Be a vessel of honor and allow God to use you every day. For every lion, there is a Samson. For every flood, there is a Noah. For every broken-down wall, there is a Nehemiah. For every Pharaoh, there is a Moses. For every Goliath, there is a David. For every Nebuchadnezzar, there is a Daniel. For every prophet of Baal, there is an Elijah. For every Jezebel, there is a Jehu. For every Herod, there is a Jesus. For every devil, there is a Holy Spirit. For every problem, there is a man of God prepared to confront it.

Problems do not arise because God has lost control; they arise because God is about to reveal a man of faith, courage, and obedience. Throughout Scripture, we see a clear pattern that when a problem appears, a man of God rises. When Israel was enslaved, Moses was born. When giants terrorized the land, David stepped forward. When Jerusalem lay in ruins, Nehemiah stood up. When idolatry ruled the nation, Elijah showed up. When salvation was needed for the world, Jesus Christ came in the fullness of time. God does not panic over problems - He positions men to solve them. A problem is not just a difficulty; it is an invitation for a man of God to take responsibility. Weak men complain. Passive men retreat. But godly men rise up, pray, act, and stand firm.

They man up! God is not looking for perfect men, He is looking for available, obedient, and courageous men who will say, "Here I am! Send me" (Is. 6:8). When everyone else sees the problem, the man of God sees an assignment.

A man of God does not run from pressure - he was built for it. He understands that authority is revealed in adversity and purpose is uncovered in opposition. The enemy brings problems to destroy; God allows problems to develop leaders. God has never changed His strategy. He still chooses men to confront darkness, restore order, and advance His kingdom. He does not outsource responsibility - He assigns it. If you see the problem, it may be because you are the man God intends to use in a powerful way. God does not reveal burdens at random. He does not allow certain injustices, needs, or broken places to trouble your spirit by accident. What disturbs you is often what calls you. What moves you is often what marks you. Many men see a need but feel nothing. They notice disorder but remain unmoved. But when a man of God encounters a problem and cannot shake it - when it lodges in his heart and refuses to leave - that is often the whisper of divine assignment.

Nehemiah saw broken walls, and others saw rubble. David saw Goliath, and others saw defeat. Moses saw oppression, and others saw normal life. The problem revealed the man. God allows certain men to *see* what others overlook because He has already placed within them the courage, faith, and resolve required to confront it. The burden is not a punishment - it is an invitation. It is God saying, "This is why I shaped you the way I did." Too many men complain about the very thing they were born to correct. They curse the darkness instead of recognizing that they were designed to carry light into that space. When God opens your eyes to a problem, He is often revealing where your authority is meant to operate. Problems expose responsibility. Vision precedes assignment. Awareness comes before action. If you see the problem clearly, it may be because you are close enough to God to hear His concern and strong enough to carry His solution.

God does not show every man every battle. He shows each man his battle. Stop asking, "Why does this bother me so much?" and start asking, "Lord, how do You want to use me here?" The man God intends to use will not always feel ready, but he will feel summoned. The discomfort you feel is not weakness; it is often evidence of an awakening, the stirring of God's purpose for your life in this matter. Discomfort is often misunderstood. We are taught to avoid it, to silence it, to escape it as quickly as possible. When God begins to stir purpose in your life, He rarely does it in a way that leaves you completely comfortable. Purpose stretches. Purpose disrupts. Purpose unsettles the familiar. The uneasiness you feel is not failure - it is God moving in your life. Before God changes your circumstances, He often disturbs your spirit. That holy discomfort is the tension between where you are and where God is calling you to go. It is the friction created when Heaven's assignment collides with earthly comfort.

If you were content to remain where you are, you might never rise to what God has placed within you. Discomfort is often God's invitation to grow. Moses felt it when he could no longer ignore the suffering of his people. David felt it when the giant mocked the armies of the living God. Nehemiah felt it when the walls of Jerusalem lay in ruins. Esther felt it when silence was no longer an option. God often allows a restlessness to stir in the hearts of those He is preparing to elevate. God does not stir discomfort to crush you; He stirs it to call you upward. The unease you carry may be God asking you to speak when you have been silent, to step forward when you have been hiding, to let go of what is familiar so you can take hold of what is eternal. What feels like internal pressure may actually be divine alignment. Do not rush to numb what God is trying to awaken. That discomfort may be the signal that you are standing at the edge of obedience, purpose, and transformation.

Throughout the Bible God moved people forward by disturbing their sense of well-being. Abraham was comfortable in Ur until God called him out. Moses was settled in the wilderness until the burning bush ignited a greater assignment. David was faithful in the fields, yet God would not let him remain unseen. None of them rose because they were satisfied to stay where they were at - they rose because they responded to God's inner stirring. Divine potential does not awaken in complacency. It awakens in holy dissatisfaction, when you refuse to settle for where you are while honoring the season you are in. God's discontent is never condemning; it is catalytic. It pushes you to pray deeper, trust harder, and step beyond what feels safe. God never designed His people to camp permanently in places meant to prepare them. Complacency dulls hunger. It whispers, "This is good enough." But divine potential responds to a deeper voice - the voice that says, "There is more, and God is calling me forward."

If God has placed something within you, He will not let you remain comfortable forever. Comfort is not the enemy, but it is never the destination. God often uses comfort as a starting place, not a staying place. When He deposits vision, calling, purpose, or destiny inside a person, that seed begins to grow and growth always creates pressure. The ache you feel is not a lack - it is a summons. Heaven is calling you upward. Holy discomfort is often the first sign that God is stirring something deeper in you. When the familiar begins to feel restrictive, when routine no longer satisfies, when rest turns into restlessness - that is not rebellion, burnout, or ingratitude. That is an awakening. Do not silence that holy discomfort. Let it drive you toward obedience, growth, and courage. Where you are may be good but what God has placed within you is far greater. Phil. 2:13 says, "For God is working in you, giving you the desire and the power to do what pleases Him."

What God places within you will eventually outgrow the environment you are in. The comfort you crave becomes too small for your calling. Comfort produces contentment while calling always produces movement. If God allowed you to remain comfortable, you might never step out in faith, confront fear, break old habits, and grow into who He created you to be. Comfort preserves the present; discomfort prepares the future. God is too loving to let you die in a place you've outgrown. This is why the tension you feel is intentional. That inner tension is not pressure from the world; it is persuasion from heaven. God will allow to be dissatisfied where you're at in life so you won't settle for less than what He has planned for you. He will disturb your peace so you will pursue His purpose. When God places something within you He will stretch you, challenge you, and call you higher. He will move you forward not to harm you but to form you into a man who will fulfill His God-given destiny.

Many men pray for peace when God is calling them to courage. They ask for rest when God is calling them to rise up. They seek comfort when God is calling them to step out. But if God has placed something within you, peace will not come from standing still and doing nothing, it will come from obeying. You must respond to the stirring inside of you. The greatest danger is not discomfort - it is ignoring it. Many people attempt to silence the very thing God is using to move them. They seek distraction instead of direction, ease instead of obedience, comfort instead of courage. But peace does not come from avoiding God's call. It comes from aligning with it. When God places something within you, the only lasting peace will be found on the other side of obedience. Embrace the calling that lies beyond your comfort. Holy discomfort is an invitation. It is God's way of saying, "There is more growth, more impact, more responsibility, more purpose."

You were not created to live a small, contained, predictable life. You were created to grow, to stretch, and to walk by faith into what God has prepared for you. If you feel uncomfortable, God may be expanding you. If you feel restless, God may be repositioning you. If you feel the pull toward something greater, God may be calling you forward. Too many men numb the stirring instead of answering it. They distract themselves, avoid responsibility, and mistake comfort for blessing. But peace does not come from avoiding God's call - it comes from obeying it. The discomfort you are trying to escape may be the very doorway God is using to lead you into the next season of your life. God is calling you up, not pushing you away. If you feel restless, God may be expanding you. If you feel challenged, God may be sharpening you. If you feel uncomfortable, God may be calling you higher. God placed something inside you that this world desperately needs. He will not let that gift remain buried beneath comfort, fear, or complacency.

God placed something within you and He intends for it to come forth. This means He will not allow you to remain comfortable forever, not because He wants you unsettled, but because He wants you fulfilled. The discomfort you feel today may be the very thing that leads you into the future He has prepared. Do not resist it. Do not fear it. Do not ignore it. Fulfillment begins when you become uncomfortable with spiritual passivity. The greatest breakthroughs in scripture never came to those who were satisfied with comfort and survival. They came to those who honored God where they were yet believed Him for where they were going. They didn't despise the wilderness but they didn't build a permanent home in it either. Do not run from discomfort - rise into it. Do not retreat - stand firm. Do not settle - step forward. God will not allow you to stay comfortable, because He did not create you to stay small. Man up. Rise up. Step into what God placed within you.

| 4 |

"A MAN OF FAITH"

God has a plan and a purpose for your life. He did not create you by accident, nor did He save you without intention. Your life has meaning for it carries divine purpose. Before you ever took a breath, God designed a plan that only you could fulfill. Scripture tells us that you are God's workmanship, created with intention, precision, and destiny (Eph. 2:10). But purpose is not fulfilled passively. God's plan for your life demands action, obedience, and courage. To walk fully in your calling as a man of God, you must man up and be bold and confident - not in yourself, but in the One who called you. Fear will always challenge purpose. Doubt will always try to silence destiny. The enemy knows that if he can keep you timid, hesitant, or insecure, you will never step into the role God prepared for you. That is why God repeatedly told His servants, "Be strong and courageous." He never said the journey would be easy, but He promised His presence would be enough.

Boldness is not arrogance. Confidence is not pride. True godly confidence flows from knowing who God is and who you are in Him. When you understand that God is for you, fear loses its authority. When you trust His plan, hesitation fades. You were not called to shrink back, you were not designed to live in uncertainty, and you were not created to hide your gifts. God needs men who will stand up and man their battle stations, men who will rise up and speak the truth no matter what the consequences may be, men who will act in faith even when they feel the enemy closing in on them. That's what courageous manhood is all about. It's when your obedience unlocks purpose, your courage activates calling, and your confidence honors the God who chose you. Man up and step forward into the plan God has for your life. Trust the plan and embrace the role God has given you. Because a man who walks boldly with God becomes exactly who God intended him to be.

Boldness and confidence come when you know God in an intimate way. Concerning God, Paul declared a powerful truth when he said in Eph. 3:12, "In Whom we have boldness and access with confidence through faith in Him." This verse reveals something remarkable about our relationship with God. Through Christ, we are not distant observers, timid servants, or fearful outsiders - we are welcomed sons. Our faith in Jesus gives us boldness, access, and confidence before God Himself. This is not arrogance or self-confidence; it is God-confidence. Biblical boldness is the courage to stand firm, pray freely, and live obediently because we know who we belong to. Fear loses its grip when faith takes its place. When you know Christ has secured your standing with God, you no longer shrink back - you man up and step forward with a willingness to do whatever it takes to get the job done, to fulfill your God-given purpose and destiny.

Under the old covenant, access to God was limited and guarded. But through Christ, the veil has been torn. We are all invited into God's presence - not occasionally, not cautiously, but continually. Prayer is no longer an act of desperation; it is a privilege. You don't need permission from man when Christ has already opened the door. Your confidence is not rooted in your performance, righteousness, or strength. It is rooted "through faith in Him." Faith anchors us in what Christ has done, not in what we fail to do. When guilt whispers, faith speaks louder. When doubt rises, faith stands firm. Confidence grows when faith trusts God's character, promises, and power. As a man of God, you are called to live from this truth - not merely believe it. Walk boldly. Pray confidently. Obey courageously. Speak truth without fear. Face challenges knowing you have full access to the wisdom, strength, and grace of God. You were never meant to approach God timidly. You were invited to come boldly, freely, and confidently because you are in Christ and He is in you.

Paul also said in 2 Tim. 1:12, "I am not ashamed, for I know Whom I have believed." Paul knew God in a deep, personal, and intimate way. For this reason, he was bold and confident just like David who told the giant, "You come to me with a sword, with a spear, and with a javelin. But I come to you in the name of the Lord of hosts" (1 Sam. 17:45). That's boldness. He then said, "This day the Lord will deliver you into my hand, and I will strike you and take your head from you."

That's confidence. When you're confident, you're bold, and when you're bold, you'll be sure that God will do what He says He will do. God did not design men to be uncertain, passive, or hesitant. A man who knows his God walks with confidence, and that confidence produces boldness. Not loud bravado. Not reckless pride. But settled strength, the kind that stands firm when pressure comes. When a man is confident in God, he becomes bold. And when he is bold, he is certain that God will do exactly what He said He would do.

Weak faith produces hesitation. Strong faith produces action. Confidence says, "I know who God is." Boldness says, "I will live like it's true." A confident man doesn't wait for perfect conditions. He steps forward because he trusts the promises of God more than the circumstances in front of him. He understands that God's word is not a suggestion - it is a guarantee. If God said it, it will happen. Bold men pray with authority, lead without fear, and obey even when obedience is costly. Fear paralyzes men who doubt God's faithfulness. But confidence destroys fear at the root. When a man is anchored in God's character, he doesn't back down, compromise, or retreat. He stands his ground because he knows heaven stands behind him. God is not looking for men who talk about faith. He is looking for men who act on it. Confidence anchors the heart of a man. Boldness directs his steps. Together, they create a life that trusts God fully and moves forward without apology.

Having confidence eliminates all doubt from your life. It allows you to forever walk in faith. Just as it is impossible to please God without faith (Heb. 11:6), it is also impossible to please

Him without confidence and boldness. Confidence brings about the death of doubt. Where confidence stands, doubt has no authority to remain. It is settled trust rooted in who God is and what He has spoken. When a man knows whom He believes, uncertainty loses its grip. Doubt thrives in hesitation, but confidence brings clarity. When confidence rises, faith becomes your way of life. You stop wavering between options and start walking with purpose. Confidence eliminates doubt because it anchors your heart. You're no longer moved by circumstances, emotions, or opposition. Storms may surround you, but they don't shake you. Pressure may come, but it doesn't break you. Why? Because your confidence isn't in outcomes - it's in God's faithfulness. You know if God is for you, nothing can stop you.

A confident man walks forward even when he cannot see the full path. He obeys before understanding. He trusts before results appear. He stands firm not because the battle is easy, but because the victory is guaranteed. When confidence rules your life, faith becomes constant. Doubt fades, fear retreats, and bold obedience becomes normal. Put your wavering and questioning aside. Don't wonder anymore and don't try to believe. Just do it! Man Up! If you are in faith, you will have confidence knowing that no weapon formed against you will prosper (Is. 54:17). Confidence doesn't just remove doubt - it establishes dominion. And a man who walks in confidence will walk in faith for a lifetime. You'll know that you know that God will move on your behalf when trials come your way. You win the good fight of faith by being sure. The word "faith" means 'to be firm, stable, to build up and support.' Faith will build under you a firm foundation. It is something you can stand on without fear of falling.

Faith is a spiritual force that you can rest your weight upon without concern that it will collapse under you. It means "to be certain, to be true, permanent, established, to believe in and to trust." Faith is not a wish, a feeling, or a hopeful guess. Faith is a spiritual force that is strong and reliable. Many people treat faith as something delicate, as though it might fail if too much pressure is placed upon it. But biblical faith was never meant to be handled carefully. It was designed to be leaned on, depended upon, and rested in without fear. True faith is like a solid foundation beneath your feet. You do not test the ground with every step, wondering if it will give way. You walk forward with confidence because you trust what is holding you up. Faith works the same way. When it is rooted in God, it does not crack under pressure, weaken in adversity, or collapse beneath the weight of your trials. Faith carries burdens, supports weary souls, and holds you steady when everything around you is shaking.

When you lean your weight on faith, you are not leaning on your own strength or understanding - you are leaning on the faithfulness of God Himself. And God has never failed to uphold those who trust in Him. The storms may rage, the winds may howl, and the ground around you may shift, but faith anchored in God remains unmovable. Resting in faith does not mean escaping responsibility; it means releasing fear. Faith allows you to stand firm without strain, to move forward without panic, and to endure without collapsing. You were never meant to carry life alone. Faith was given so you could place the full weight of your worries, decisions, and future upon God without concern that He will fail you. When you place your full weight on God, you discover something powerful - He does not shift, strain, or stumble. He remains the same yesterday, today, and forever. What feels heavy to you is effortless to Him. Lean on faith. Depend on faith. Rest your weight upon it for it will surely hold you up.

A man of faith is never meant to be timid. Faith and fear cannot occupy the same heart. When faith rises, boldness follows because faith anchors the soul in the certainty of God, not the opinions of people or the threat of circumstances. Boldness does not mean arrogance, loudness, or recklessness. True spiritual boldness is quiet confidence rooted in trust. It is the courage to stand when others retreat, to speak when silence would be safer, and to obey even when the outcome is uncertain. Faith gives a person backbone. It replaces hesitation with conviction. A bold man who is strong and courageous understands that God is forever at his side. That awareness changes everything. When you know you are not alone, fear loses its hold on you. When you trust that God goes before you, obstacles become opportunities to witness His power. Faith does not deny danger; it simply refuses to bow to it. Bold faith moves forward and walks through open doors without fear of what's on the other side.

When you man up you will believe that God's promises are stronger than your circumstances and His Word more reliable than your feelings. A man of faith may feel fear, but he does not live under it and will never let it stop him. Boldness is faith in action. It is faith with legs, faith with a voice, faith that refuses to hide. When a man truly believes God, he will no longer shrink back. He will man up because faith does not produce cowards. Faith speaks boldly and produces courage. And because your confidence is in God, you can speak openly and freely with no uncertainty in your heart. This is what David did when he faced Goliath. There is no need to soften truth, hide conviction, or speak with trembling. Faith removes the double-minded heart and establishes a firm resolve. When God has spoken to you, uncertainty has no place to remain. When your confidence is anchored in God, courage rises naturally within your heart causing you to say what needs to be said and do what needs to be done.

Faith does not produce hesitation - it produces boldness. It settles the inner debate and replaces uncertainty with assurance. Faith gives you confidence in the faithfulness of God. And when your trust is fully placed in Him, fear loses its authority. Courage is not the absence of fear - it is the presence of trust. Faith produces a bold spirit that speaks without apology and stands without wavering. It allows you to declare what God has promised even when circumstances disagree. Faith speaks from assurance, not from pressure. When your heart is settled in God, your voice becomes steady. When your trust is complete, your words carry authority. And when faith is alive within you, courage flows naturally; clear, confident, and unashamed. Let your faith speak. Let your confidence remain in God. And let your heart be free from uncertainty because the One you trust never fails. You are unstoppable when you are bold and have confidence in God. For sure, no enemy can stop you from going all the way with God.

Heb. 10:35 says, "Therefore do not cast away your confidence, which has great reward." This verse does not tell you to find confidence, but to keep it. That means confidence is already yours, placed within you by faith. At the same time, it must be guarded. Life has a way of pressuring men to loosen their grip on confidence. Delays test it. Opposition challenges it. Weariness whispers that surrender would be easier. But the Bible tells you plainly to not throw it away. Confidence is not expendable - it is valuable. Heaven calls it precious because it carries a great reward. That reward is more than future blessing; it is present strength. Confidence steadies your steps when the path is uncertain. It gives you boldness to pray, courage to obey, and endurance to remain faithful when results are unseen. It is confidence that anchors your soul, reminding you that God's faithfulness is not altered by circumstances. To cast away confidence is to forget the proven goodness of God.

Faith that endures is faith that remembers. It remembers past deliverance, present grace, and promised victory. So stand firm. Hold your ground. Refuse to let fear, doubt, or delay rob you of what God has already deposited within you. Your confidence is not misplaced, and it will not return empty. The reward is coming, and the strength to wait is part of the gift. Hold fast. Stay confident. God is faithful and He always finishes what He starts. Because of that, you can boldly have confidence that good things will happen in your life. Scripture tells us that God delights in blessing His children and leading them into hope, peace, and purpose. When you believe this, your outlook changes. You no longer wait for life to improve before you rejoice. You rejoice because you know God is already at work behind the scenes. Bold faith stands firm with confidence that God's promises will come to pass at the appointed time. This assurance fills your heart with peace and your steps with courage.

When your faith is strong, your expectation is strong. You can wake up each day believing that God is ordering your steps, opening doors, and causing good things to unfold in your life. Confidence anchored in faith gives you the freedom to be hopeful, joyful, and unafraid trusting that what God has promised, He will surely perform. Don't be passive, be possessive! Passivity has quietly robbed many believers of ground God already gave them. It convinces you to wait when you should advance, to tolerate what you should confront, and to accept less than what God promised. But faith was never meant to sit back, it was designed to take hold. God's promises are not trophies placed on a shelf; they are inheritances to be possessed. God is saying to you, "Rise up for every place the sole of your foot treads, I have given you." Possession requires movement. It requires courage. It requires resolve. 1 Tim. 6:12 (MSG) says, "Run hard and fast in the faith. Seize the eternal life, the life you were called to."

The Greek word for "seize" means 'take.' With confidence that is sure and bold, you need to man up and take by faith what God says you can have. He is not looking for men who are passive but men who trust Him enough to act on His Word without apology. The promises of God were written to be taken by faith. When God says you can have the blessing, He is calling for you to go forth and take it. This is obedient confidence. It is faith that knows who God is and who it belongs to. Biblical faith is bold certainty. It stands flat-footed on the Word of God and refuses to retreat even when circumstances push back. Faith moves forward because God has already spoken. Every promise of God requires a man willing to step forward and claim it. Canaan was promised, but it still had to be possessed. Victory was spoken, but it still required courage. The blessing was given, but it had to be taken. Timidity never conquered a giant. Hesitation never claimed an inheritance. Doubt never built a legacy.

The bottom line is when God says walk, you walk. When He says take, you take. So man up. Stand firm. Be bold. Take by faith what God has already declared belongs to you. The kingdom of God advances through men who take what rightfully belongs to them. Possessive faith prays boldly, speaks decisively, and acts deliberately. It lays hold of truth, clings to righteousness, and presses forward even when resistance comes. Stop waiting for permission to walk in what God already authorized. Take responsibility for your spiritual life. Take ownership of God's Word. Take possession of the promises spoken over you. The battle is not won by the passive observer, but by the faithful possessor. Men who possess the promises are not weak and passive, they're bold and aggressive. God provides what you need and want but you must rise up and possess it. You must possess your possessions. Don't be passive. Be possessive. What God gave you is worth fighting for. If you don't take it, you won't get it!

| 5 |

"THE DAY OF ADVERSITY"

All men were created to solve problems. That's right. Every man was created with purpose - not by accident, not as an afterthought, and not to drift through life reacting to circumstances. God designed men to identify problems, confront them, and bring order where chaos exists. That is why you are here. From the beginning, God placed Adam in the garden not merely to enjoy it, but to tend it and keep it. That assignment required responsibility, awareness, and action. Problems were not a curse - they were the environment in which purpose would be revealed. A man discovers who he is not in comfort, but in confrontation. You were wired to think, to build, to protect, to lead, and to overcome. When something is broken, incomplete, or out of alignment, something inside you is supposed to rise. That inner stirring is not frustration - it is calling. Problems awaken the gifts God placed within you long before you faced the challenge.

The world does not need more men who run from difficulty, blame others, or wait to be rescued. It needs men who man up

51

and say, "This is why I'm here. I was created to fix this." You are not here just to survive problems, you are here to solve them with wisdom, courage, faith, and obedience to God. Problems are not proof you are out of place. They are proof you are right where you belong. God never calls a man to live for himself alone. From the beginning, the calling of a godly man has always been outward, not inward. He is called to stand, serve, and strengthen the lives of others. As a man of God, your calling is to man up and help make the lives of other people better. To do that, you must be strong and mighty, engulfed with spiritual power. 2 Cor. 10:4 says, "The weapons of our warfare are not carnal but mighty in God for pulling down strongholds." The stronger you are spiritually, the more you can resist the devil and be in a position to help other people.

Serving God and working in the ministry is hard work and you must continually be building up your inner man. Serving God is not light work. Ministry is not a weekend hobby or a casual calling - it is labor of the soul. Those who answer the call soon discover that the work of God presses not only on the hands, but deeply on the heart, the mind, and the spirit. Scripture never pretends otherwise. 1 Cor. 3:9 says, "We are laborers together with God." Labor implies effort. It implies strain. It implies days when obedience costs more than convenience and faith must stand when feelings fail. The call to ministry is a call to endurance. Gal. 6:9 says, "Let us not grow weary in well doing for in due season we will reap if we faint not." Fainting does not begin in the body - it begins in the spirit. That is why God commands us to guard, feed, and build the inner man continually. The strongest men of God are those who have learned to kneel in private, weep in prayer, and rise strengthened in spirit.

If ministry feels heavy, it does not mean you are failing, it means you are laboring. Don't forget that God never called you to carry the weight alone. He called you to be strengthened with might by His Spirit in the inner man (Eph. 3:16). Paul is saying you need a strong spirit to do the things God would have you do. In other words, you need to Man Up! Strong faith comes from having a strong spirit. Faith is not merely agreeing with truth; it is standing on truth when circumstances try to shake you loose. And the strength of that stand is directly tied to the strength of your inner spirit. A weak spirit will believe God only when things are easy. A strong spirit believes God even when everything says otherwise. The spirit in your inner man is the core of who we are. It's the place where conviction lives, where courage is born, and where trust in God takes root. When the spirit is neglected, faith becomes fragile. But when the spirit is nourished, faith becomes unshakable.

Strong faith grows out of time spent with God, obedience, and great endurance. Every trial you endure, every temptation you resist, and every act of obedience strengthens your spirit. And as your spirit grows stronger, so does your ability to trust God without wavering. A strong spirit does not panic in storms. A strong spirit does not collapse under pressure, nor does it retreat when challenged. Instead, it stands firm because it is anchored in God's promises and is confident in His faithfulness. Faith is not strengthened by avoiding hardship but by overcoming it with God. Just as muscles grow through resistance, faith grows when the spirit refuses to quit. The stronger the spirit, the steadier the faith. If you desire strong faith, invest in your spirit. Feed it with truth. Guard it from compromise. Exercise it through obedience. Strengthen it through perseverance. Because when your spirit is strong, your faith will not fail. When trials come, be like Paul who said, "None of these things move me" (Acts 20:24).

Paul understood a very powerful truth that when your life is surrendered to God's purpose, circumstances lose their power to control you. He had counted the cost and decided that obedience was worth more than ease, that faithfulness mattered more than survival, and that finishing God's will outweighed preserving his own comfort. Storms may rage. Opposition may rise. Losses may come. But when your heart is fixed on God's calling, you are no longer easily shaken. Yes, Paul felt pain. He knew sorrow. He faced danger. But he refused to let any of it redirect his devotion. Being unmoved does not mean you feel nothing - it means you refuse to let feelings rule your faith. Faith that stands firm says, "I will not be moved by fear, criticism, and suffering." In a world that constantly pressures believers to compromise, Paul's words ring louder than ever. God is still looking for men who will man up and say, "No matter what comes, none of these things move me."

When you man up you'll be a warrior whose loyalty cannot be shaken, whose mission cannot be derailed, and whose faith is stronger than the trials you face. When your eyes are fixed on Christ and your life is yielded to His will, you too can stand firm against the evil forces that try to take you down. Don't let things move your heart or shake your confidence. Prov. 24:10 says, "If you faint in the day of adversity, your strength is small." Adversity is not sent to destroy you; it is allowed to reveal who you are. When pressure comes, it exposes what lies beneath the surface of your faith. Comfort can hide weakness, but hardship brings truth into the light. This proverb is not an insult; it is an invitation. God is not mocking those who struggle, He is calling His people to grow stronger. The "day of adversity" is inevitable. Trials will come. Opposition will rise. Delays, disappointments, and attacks will test every believer. The real question is not if adversity will come, but how you respond when it does.

To faint means to lose heart, to quit inwardly before the battle is finished. Many don't fall because the problem was too big but because their inner strength was too small. Strength is not measured by words spoken in peace, but by endurance displayed in pressure. Spiritual strength is built before the storm arrives. It is forged through prayer, obedience, discipline, and trust in God's Word. When adversity comes, it draws from what has already been deposited within. A shallow faith collapses quickly, but a rooted faith stands firm. God desires His men to be resilient, steadfast, unmovable, and confident in Him. The day of adversity is not proof of God's absence; it is often the stage where His power is meant to be demonstrated in you and through you. If adversity has caused you to faint, do not despair. Instead, strengthen what remains. Return to the Word. Renew your mind. Rebuild your inner man. The same God who allows the test also supplies the strength to overcome it.

Adversity does not define you - your response does. Stand strong and let every trial become proof that your strength in God is increasing. The evidence of a weak spirit is despair and discouragement. There is no such thing as a strong spirit that is down and depressed. Prov. 14:18 says, "The spirit of a man will sustain him in infirmity." When trials come you are to man up and "be strong in the Lord and in the power of His might" (Eph. 6:10). The NLT says, "Be strong with the Lord's mighty power." Strength in the kingdom of God does not begin with muscle, confidence, or self-discipline. True strength begins when you recognize your weakness and turn fully toward the Lord. The Lord's mighty power is divine authority at work in human lives. When you rely on God's strength, you are no longer limited by your natural abilities or past failures. His power sustains you when you are weary, steadies you when you are afraid, and empowers you to stand firm when everything around you is shaking.

To be strong in the Lord means you draw your confidence from His faithfulness, not your circumstances. It means you trust His Word even when emotions waver. It means you stand our ground - not in pride or anger - but in humble dependence on God's truth. His strength equips you to resist temptation, endure hardship, and walk in obedience when the path is difficult. The mighty power of the Lord renews the mind, strengthens the heart, and shapes the inner man. Through His power, fear gives way to courage, doubt bows to faith, and weakness is exchanged for perseverance. God does not simply help you to survive; He empowers you to overcome. When you put on the Lord's strength, you are clothed with spiritual authority. You are able to stand against the schemes of the enemy, not because you are intimidating, but because God is. His power goes before you, surrounds you, and works within you producing steadfast faith and unshakable hope.

You are an overcomer, and victory is inside of you. The power that raised Christ from the dead lives inside of you, and that means defeat does not get the final word. Circumstances may press in, voices may try to weaken your resolve, and challenges may seem overwhelming, but victory lives within you. You overcome not because you are flawless, but because Christ is faithful. Every trial you face is already met with heaven's strength. When the enemy says, "You're finished," God says, "You're just getting started." What rises against you will not remain, because the Spirit of God within you is greater than anything that comes against you. You carry overcoming power in your faith, courage in your obedience, and endurance in your hope. Even when you stumble, you rise up because overcomers don't quit. They stand. They believe. They move forward. Victory is not the absence of struggle; it is the presence of God sustaining you through it. You're a strong and mighty warrior so act like it and talk like it.

Your actions and your words must agree with who God says you are. Too many men carry the armor of God but talk like civilians. They pray for victory while rehearsing defeat. They ask God for strength while confessing weakness. But warriors understand that what you speak shapes how you walk. You don't win battles by complaining about how hard they are. You don't overcome giants by announcing how small you feel. You overcome by declaring God's truth over your life especially when you don't feel it yet. Act like a warrior and stand firm when pressure comes. Advance forward when fear tells you to retreat and endure with confidence when quitting feels easier. Talk like a warrior. Speak faith instead of fear, truth instead of doubt, victory instead of defeat. Your words should sound like someone who knows God is with them, someone who knows they were built for battle, someone who understands that strength is not just in muscles but in conviction, obedience, and courage.

You must feed your spirit if your spirit is going to be strong. Strength does not come from wishing, hoping, or surviving - it comes from feeding. Just as your body weakens without food, your spirit withers when it is starved. You cannot live on yesterday's prayer, last week's word, or someone else's faith. A hungry spirit becomes tired, fearful, confused, and easily defeated. But a fed spirit becomes bold, steady, discerning, and unshakable. Always remember that what you feed grows, what you neglect weakens. If you constantly feed your flesh but starve your spirit, you will feel powerless even though you are called to be strong. The battles of life are not won with natural strength alone; they are won with spiritual strength, and spiritual strength is built daily. Your spirit is fed through the Word of God, which renews your mind and sharpens your inner man, prayer which connects you to heaven's power, worship which realigns your heart with truth, and obedience which keeps your spirit clean and sensitive.

When you feed your spirit, something changes. Fear loses its grip, faith rises naturally, discernment becomes clearer, and endurance replaces weariness. A strong spirit does not panic in pressure and does not quit in adversity. It stands firm when everything else shakes. If you feel weak, don't condemn yourself - check your diet. Nourishment for the inner man is the Word of God. 1 Peter 2:2 says, "Desire the pure milk of the Word, that you may grow thereby. Job 23:12 says, "I have treasured the words of His mouth more than my necessary food." Feed your spirit every day with God's Word and build yourself up. As you read and meditate on the Word you will feel strength coming into you. Your spirit is getting developed and becoming strong and mighty. You were never created to live spiritually malnourished. You were created to be strong, alert, and full of life. Feed your spirit daily, and it will carry you through every battle, every storm, and every calling placed on your life.

Real men never give up! They conquer one mountain and then go climb another one. You can do the same because you are a champion, a master, a winner! You know that real men don't quit when the climb gets steep. They don't lay down when the wind howls or the trail disappears. A real man understands that giving up is not an option when God has called you forward. He conquers one mountain and, instead of settling in comfort, he lifts his eyes and finds the next peak. Why? Because growth never stops, purpose never retires, and faith is meant to be exercised, not shelved. Every mountain represents a fear to overcome, a weakness to discipline, a calling to answer, and a promise to pursue. The summit isn't the end

- it's proof that God carried you through and prepared you for more. Real men don't brag at the top; they bow in gratitude, tighten their boots, and move again. A quitter looks for relief. A conqueror looks for another assignment, another mountain to climb and conquer.

Real men know that strength is forged in resistance, courage is proven in persistence, and victory belongs to those who keep climbing even when their legs burn and their lungs ache. So if you've just conquered a mountain - don't get comfortable. Lift your head. Set your eyes higher. There's another mountain waiting, and you were built to climb it. We are at war with the forces of evil and Matt. 11:12 says, "The kingdom of God is advancing forcefully, and forceful men lay hold of it." The kingdom of God is not passive, fragile, or reserved for the spiritually timid. Jesus declares that God's kingdom is advancing with force, and it is seized by men who are bold, resolved, and spiritually aggressive. This verse does not glorify violence - it calls for holy determination. The kingdom advances whenever truth confronts darkness, righteousness challenges compromise, and faith refuses to retreat. Forceful men are alive and well and refuse to settle for shallow faith, casual obedience, or comfortable Christianity.

Real men press in when others pull back. They pray when resistance rises. They obey even when obedience costs them everything. To lay hold of the kingdom means to take responsibility for your spiritual life. It means fighting complacency, resisting temptation, and standing firm against fear. The enemy does not yield ground willingly, and neither should the man of God. Spiritual inheritance is claimed by those who refuse to let go of the call on their life. This kind of force is faith with backbone. It is repentance that breaks pride, obedience that defies pressure, and courage that endures persecution. Heaven responds to men who will not be moved on the day of adversity. The kingdom is advancing today. The question is not whether God is moving - the question is whether you will move with Him. Now is the time to man up and hold your ground against the forces of evil, the time to lay hold of what God has already made available. For sure, the kingdom belongs to those who refuse to be passive.

| 6 |

"WIN FROM WITHIN"

We live in a world at war and as a man of God you're supposed to fight back. This means that the time to man up is now! Whether we acknowledge it or not, the battlefield surrounds us. There is no neutral territory in this war. Silence is not safety. Passivity is not peace. If you are not advancing, you are retreating. The enemy understands this well, which is why he works tirelessly to keep men distracted, divided, discouraged, and disengaged. He knows that a passive man is a defeated man. Understand that this war is personal. It targets the very core of who you are as a man. Your mind is under attack through deception, compromise, and confusion. Your heart is under siege through bitterness, lust, fear, and weariness. Your home is a target through broken leadership, moral collapse, and spiritual neglect. God never intended His men to live this way. From the beginning, God designed men to guard, lead, and protect. Strength was never meant to be used for domination, but for responsibility.

The calling of a man of God is not comfort; it is faithful resistance against evil. Fighting back does not mean rage or recklessness. It means discipline. It means refusing to surrender ground God has given you. It means standing firm when it would be easier to bow. A man of God fights first on his knees, but he does not stay on the ground; he rises ready to stand and fight. This war demands engagement. It demands alertness. It demands men who are willing to say, "As for me, I will not retreat, and I will not surrender." There is a heavy price to pay for passivity. When men refuse to fight, others pay the price. Families suffer, churches weaken, and truth becomes negotiable. Passivity is not harmless; it is destructive. A passive man may avoid confrontation, but he does not avoid the consequences of it. What a man fails to confront today will confront him tomorrow with greater force and deeper cost. The enemy thrives when men refuse to lead, when they choose comfort over courage.

This is the moment to man up - not in arrogance, but in accountability; not in pride, but in purpose; not in aggression, but in authority under God. To man up means to accept responsibility for your spiritual life. It means to confront sin instead of coddling it. It means to lead your home instead of leaving it vulnerable. It means to stand in truth when culture pressures you to conform. God is not calling men to be loud; He is calling them to be faithful. He is not searching for flawless men, but for men who are willing to fight for righteousness regardless of the cost. This war cannot be won with good intentions alone. It requires preparation. A man of God must be grounded in truth, disciplined in obedience, and committed to holiness. Prayer becomes his lifeline. The Word becomes his weapon. Obedience becomes his strength. Every day presents a choice: to suit up or sit down. Engage or withdraw. Stand or surrender. There is no victory without resistance. There is no crown without a battle.

The world does not need more passive men. It does not need men who blend in or bow down. It needs men who know who they are, whose they are, and why they were called. You were not created to survive the war - you were created to stand in it. This sinful world is your battlefield and making it a better place is your assignment. Now is not the time to retreat. Now is not the time to hesitate. Now is the time to man up, fight back, and stand firm in the calling God has placed on your life. God hates cowardice and Rev. 21:8 says cowards are the first who are thrown into hell. In one sweeping judgment scene, God lists the kinds of people who will be excluded from His eternal kingdom. Shockingly, the list does not begin with murderers or the sexually immoral. It begins with the cowardly. That verse is not accidental. God is communicating something essential to men everywhere, that cowardice is not weakness, it is unbelief in action and should be avoided at all costs.

Cowardice is rarely preached about, yet scripture speaks of it with sobering force. In an age that excuses fear, celebrates safety, and rewards silence, the Bible draws a hard line. God does not treat cowardice as a minor flaw or a harmless personality trait. He treats it as a spiritual condition with eternal consequences. To understand why God condemns cowardice so strongly, we must define it biblically. Cowardice is not the experience of fear. Every human being feels fear, including God's servants. Moses feared Pharaoh. Elijah feared Jezebel. Even Jesus experienced anguish in the Garden of Gethsemane. Cowardice is not feeling fear - it is allowing fear to rule your obedience. Biblical cowardice occurs when a person knows what God requires yet refuses to act because obedience carries risk. It is fear elevated above faith. It is retreat disguised as caution. It is silence masquerading as wisdom. Fear that governs behavior reveals a heart that does not fully trust God.

God hates cowardice because it contradicts His nature. God is not passive. God is not timid. God does not retreat. He speaks, acts, confronts, and overcomes. When He created mankind, He placed within all men the expectation to reflect His character. Scripture declares plainly that God has not given His people a spirit of fear. Fear that controls decision-making does not come from Him. It comes from the flesh, from the world, or from the enemy. Cowardice insults God by declaring that He is not sufficient to protect, sustain, or vindicate those who obey Him. It suggests that the threat before us is greater than the God who stands behind us. That is why cowardice is never neutral. It always sides against faith. Throughout Scripture, God consistently calls His people to stand when retreat is easier, to stand when the culture shifts, when truth is unpopular, and when obedience costs reputation, relationships, or comfort. Cowardice refuses this call. It draws back. It compromises. It hides. It blends in.

Scripture warns repeatedly about those who "draw back." Faith presses forward. Fear withdraws. God takes no pleasure in those who retreat when truth demands courage. History bears witness to this pattern. When giants appear cowards calculate odds, but men of faith move forward. When laws forbid righteousness, cowards comply but the faithful remain unmoved. When silence is rewarded, cowards keep quiet but the bold speak anyway. God has never advanced His purposes through fearful people. Courage does not mean the absence of fear. Courage means obedience in the presence of fear. It is the decision to trust God more than circumstances, consequences, or comfort. The righteous are called bold, not because they are reckless, but because they believe God is faithful. Courage flows from confidence in who God is and what He has promised. Faith that never risks obedience is not faith at all. Faith moves. Faith speaks. Faith stands. When courage is embraced, God is glorified.

God is raising up men who will fight back, men who stand unashamed, unmoved, and unafraid; not because they are strong, but because they trust a strong God. You were not created to shrink back; you were not redeemed to remain silent, and you were not called to blend in. God is worthy of your courage so fight back and stand, speak, and obey knowing it is God's will that all cowards be gone from His kingdom. This is why Deut. 31:6 gives the command to "be strong and courageous, do not fear nor be afraid of them." You are stronger than your enemy because God has made you stronger. The battle you are facing is not evidence of your weakness; it is proof of your strength. You do not attract resistance because you are fragile. You attract it because God has made you strong. The enemy does not waste time fighting what is already defeated. He targets what carries purpose, authority, and power. If you are under attack, it is not because you are losing; it is because you are dangerous.

God never calls His warriors to fight in their own strength. He calls them to stand in His. Ps. 28:7 says, "The Lord is my strength and my shield; my heart trusted in Him, and I am helped." Your strength is not emotional confidence or physical ability. It is not willpower or personality. Your strength flows from the unchanging power of God working within you. What God supplies cannot be drained, diminished, or exhausted. The enemy thrives on intimidation. He wants you to believe the lie that you are outmatched, overwhelmed, and outnumbered. But heaven does not measure battles the way earth does. When David stood before Goliath, the size of the enemy was irrelevant. What mattered was who stood behind David. God does not merely encourage you - He equips you. He does not simply comfort you - He fortifies you. When God strengthens a person, He reinforces them from the inside out. Ps. 29:11 says, "The Lord gives strength to His people; the Lord blesses His people with peace."

This strength is not always loud. Sometimes it looks like endurance. Sometimes it looks like obedience when quitting would be easier. Sometimes it looks like standing still while the enemy exhausts himself. Do not mistake calm for weakness. Do not mistake patience for passivity. Do not mistake silence for surrender. God's strength is steady, immovable, and unshakable. The enemy fights you because he cannot dominate you. He pressures you because he cannot possess you. He resists you because he fears what God is producing in you. He knows that if you remain standing, his defeat is only a matter of time. James 4:7 says, "Resist the devil, and he will flee from you." Notice you are to resist the devil. You don't panic, retreat, or negotiate. Resistance is not aggression, it is confidence. It is knowing who you belong to and refusing to move. The enemy's power depends on deception. Once the truth takes root that God has made you stronger, the enemy's advantage disappears.

You are not fighting alone. You never have been. Rom. 8:11 says, "The Spirit of Him who raised Jesus from the dead dwells in you." The same Spirit that raised Christ from the dead lives in you. That truth alone settles every argument about who is stronger. God is in you! Inside of you is the spirit of a warrior. This means you "win from within." 1 John 4:4 says, "Greater is He that is in you, than he that is in the world." This means you have a strength that gives you peace, stability, and assurance. The enemy may roar, but God reigns. The enemy may threaten, but God rules. The enemy may strike, but God sustains. You are strengthened by the One who cannot be defeated. Ex. 15:3 says, "The Lord is a man of war; The Lord is His name." Is. 42:13 says, "The Lord shall go forth like a mighty man; He shall stir up His zeal like a man of war." God made you a warrior in His own image because He intends for you to join Him in the battle. Eph. 6:10 says, "Be strong in the Lord and in the power of His might."

Victory does not come from striving harder - it comes from standing firmer. When you rely on God's strength, fear loses its grip, doubt loses its voice, and intimidation loses its power. God's strength does not make you reckless; it makes you resolute. It does not make you arrogant; it makes you anchored. You no longer react to the enemy's noise because you are rooted in God's truth. You stand not because you feel strong but because God has made you strong. The enemy's goal is to wear you down, but he cannot wear out what God renews. Every attempt against you will fail. Every scheme will collapse. Every attack will turn into testimony. Is. 54:17 says, "No weapon formed against you shall prosper." God has already spoken the outcome. You are not fighting for victory - you are standing in it. So lift your head, set your feet, and strengthen your heart. You are stronger than your enemy not because of who you are, but because of who your God is. And what God strengthens, no enemy can defeat.

David wrote in Ps. 24:8, "Who is the King of glory? The Lord strong and mighty, the Lord mighty in battle." Our God is not distant, passive, or unsure. He is not a silent observer of human struggle. He is a warrior King, proven in conflict and victorious in every engagement. From the beginning, the Lord has revealed Himself as One who steps into the fight against chaos, darkness, sin, and fear and emerges undefeated. The strength of the Lord is not reckless force; it is holy power governed by righteousness. His might is not for oppression, but for deliverance. When Scripture calls Him "mighty in battle," it declares that there has never been a war He could not win, a foe He could not defeat, or a burden He could not lift from His people. This truth changes how we face life's battles. We do not fight alone. We do not rely on our own strength, wisdom, or endurance. The King of glory goes before us. He fights for us. He stands over us as Protector and Champion. What overwhelms us does not overwhelm Him.

Life is a battle, a struggle, and there is no such thing as an easy life. To win the battle, you must rise above your circumstances and be the victor instead of the victim. You do not overcome by sinking into your circumstances - you overcome by rising above them. Circumstances are temporary, but truth is eternal. Fear, pressure, loss, and opposition may shout loudly, but they do not have the final word. When you rise above what you see and anchor yourself in faith, you shift from reacting to reigning. You stop asking, "Why is this happening to me?" and begin declaring, "This will not conquer me." A victim waits for rescue. A victor moves forward with authority. Rising above does not mean denying the battle - it means refusing to be controlled by it. It is choosing faith over feelings, purpose over pain, and courage over comfort. The higher your perspective, the smaller the obstacle becomes. You were not called to be crushed by adversity but strengthened through it.

Every challenge is an invitation to man up and think higher, speak stronger, and walk bolder. When you rise above your circumstances, you step into the position of victory that was already prepared for you. The battle is won from higher ground so throw off the cloak of passivity and put on the whole armor of God. Too many believers fight from the valley where they're reactive, weary, and exposed when God has already called them to rise. Eph. 2:6 says God "has raised us up together and made us sit in heavenly places in Christ Jesus." Passivity is not humility. Passivity is surrender without obedience. The enemy loves passivity because it requires no resistance. A passive believer delays, tolerates, excuses, and avoids confrontation while darkness advances unhindered. Passivity disguises itself as patience, but it produces spiritual paralysis. You were never meant to fight from below; you were designed to fight from above so man up knowing that to kill the lion you've got to run to the roar!

Every man will face a roar. It may come as fear, pressure, temptation, opposition, or responsibility. It announces itself loudly, confidently, and without apology. The roar is designed to intimidate you, to make you pause, hesitate, and question whether you are truly capable of what lies before you. Most men step back when they hear it. They rationalize. They wait. They hope the noise will fade on its own. But the roar never fades. It only grows louder the longer it is ignored. Here is the hard truth: you do not defeat the lion by running from its roar. You defeat it by charging straight toward it. The battlefield is always a valley. Valleys are low places - places of exposure where there is nowhere to hide. In the Valley of Elah, the army of Israel stood paralyzed. Goliath's voice echoed day after day, dripping with threats and mockery. The men who were trained for war, armored for battle, and experienced in combat refused to move. Then a young shepherd boy arrived.

David did not look like a warrior. He did not carry the weapons of a king. But he carried something far more dangerous. He had unshakable confidence in God. When David heard the roar, it did not frighten him; it offended him. The giant was not merely challenging Israel - he was defying the living God. And David knew something the others had forgotten: the size of the enemy does not determine the outcome of the battle. The presence of God does. Scripture tells us that when the moment came, David ran toward the giant. He did not inch forward. He did not pause to reconsider. He ran. David did not wait for permission. He did not ask for consensus. He did not need approval from fearful men. Faith does not wait for ideal conditions. Faith moves when God speaks. David had already faced lions and bears in private places, long before the public battle ever appeared. He learned that God is faithful in the shadows so that a man can be fearless in the spotlight.

To man up does not mean to rely on brute strength. It means to stand in confidence, grounded in truth, unafraid of confrontation. It means refusing to be ruled by fear, noise, or intimidation. The roar is not random. It is a signal that points directly to what must be confronted. The thing that frightens you the most is often the very thing standing between you and your next level of obedience. The roar identifies the battle that matters. Responsibility roars. Calling roars. Conviction roars. And every time you turn away from it, the roar grows louder. The lion roars to intimidate, but it also exposes itself. A roaring lion is no longer hidden. It reveals its position. The man who understands this does not run away - he locks his eyes on the source and moves forward. The roar wants you to believe that you are not enough. But when God is with you, enough is irrelevant. You do not need perfect confidence. You need obedience that moves forward despite fear. The giant falls when the man of God advances.

Men retreat for many reasons. Some retreat because of fear of failure, fear of rejection, fear of being exposed as inadequate. Others retreat because of comfort. It is easier to remain where you are than to face what demands growth. But often, men retreat because they have forgotten who they are. The roar convinces a man that he is small, weak, and unprepared. It magnifies the problem until God looks distant and irrelevant. The enemy knows that if he can keep you standing still, he has already won. Standing still is defeat disguised as caution. Every generation needs men who run toward the roar instead of away from it, men who step into responsibility when others shrink back, men who confront sin instead of excusing it, men who lead when leadership is costly. The roar is loud because it is afraid of what happens when you move. Pick up your sling and plant your feet in faith. David ran toward the giant, and you must do the same. God in you will make you stronger than whatever trial you are facing.

| 7 |

"MEN OF ACTION"

You are a warrior, and you are called to win major battles in life. You win beside God is on your side. Ps. 121:1,2 says, "I lift my eyes to the hills. Where does my help come from? My help comes from the Lord, the Maker of heaven and earth." The psalmist looks to the hills, not because the hills hold the answer, but because they remind him that help must come from beyond himself. The hills represent strength, stability, and refuge but even they are not enough. The psalmist quickly redirects his gaze higher. Help does not come from people, money, influence, or personal strength. Help comes from the One who created all of those things. 1 John 4:4 says, "He who is in you is greater than he who is in the world." Jesus said in Luke 10:19, "Behold, I give you the authority to trample on serpents and scorpions, and over all the power of the enemy, and nothing shall by any means hurt you." Warriors believe that, cowards don't.

Webster's Dictionary defines "courage" as 'the attitude of facing and dealing with anything recognized as dangerous, difficult, or painful.' Warriors run toward danger because they know God is on their side. Warriors eat problems for breakfast, lunch, and supper. They do it for fun. They look at every problem as a set of weights that will help them grow stronger. This is why a warrior does not flee when danger rises. A warrior moves forward not because the threat is small, but because God is great. Fear causes ordinary men to retreat, but faith causes warriors to advance. When danger appears, the warrior's eyes are not fixed on the size of the enemy, the strength of the opposition, or the intensity of the storm. His eyes are fixed on the God who stands beside him. True warriors know a secret the fearful do not: God does not abandon His people in battle - He enters the battle with them. A warrior runs toward danger because he knows God goes before him, stands with him, and fights for him.

Throughout Scripture, God's warriors ran toward danger because they understood this truth. David ran toward Goliath, not with confidence in his sling, but with confidence in the name of the Lord. Joshua marched into fortified cities because God had already promised victory. Gideon faced overwhelming odds knowing that obedience mattered more than numbers. Danger does not signal defeat - it signals opportunity. It is the place where God reveals His power, His faithfulness, and His glory. When a warrior charges forward in faith, heaven responds. Running toward danger does not mean recklessness - it means trust. It means believing that obedience is safer than retreat, and faith is stronger than fear. The warrior understands that even if the battle is fierce, the outcome is already secure in God's hands. God did not call His warriors to hide, hesitate, or shrink back. He called them to man up. Warriors don't run from danger. They run toward it carrying faith, courage, and the presence of God into the fight.

Danger is your opportunity to awaken courage. Courage sleeps quietly until it is awakened by an opportunity to confront danger head-on. Danger has a way of interrupting life without asking permission. It arrives suddenly, shakes the ground beneath your feet, and demands a response. In those moments, we often pray for danger to leave as quickly as it came. Comfort can soothe the soul, but it rarely builds courage. Ease may calm the heart, but it does not sharpen faith. Danger exposes what comfort conceals. It strips away false confidence and reveals what you truly trust. When the threat is real and the outcome uncertain, belief moves from theory to action. It is in danger that courage is born, not because fear is absent, but because faith refuses to retreat. Courage is not the absence of fear; it is obedience in the presence of fear, the decision to stand anyway. Scripture reminds us that God has not given us a spirit of fear, but of power, love, and a sound mind (2 Tim. 1:7).

That power is not passive. It is not decorative. It is activated under pressure. Fear reveals itself in danger but so does faith. And when faith rises, courage follows. Throughout the Word of God, danger consistently precedes breakthrough. David did not discover his courage tending sheep; it awakened when a giant mocked the armies of the living God. Daniel's faith was proven not in prayer meetings alone, but in a den filled with lions. Esther's courage did not emerge in comfort, but when silence meant death and speaking meant risk. In every case, danger forced a decision. Do you retreat and run away, or do you man up and run to the battle? God does not waste threats. He uses them to refine leaders, awaken warriors, and expose the strength of the inner man. What looks like an obstacle is often an invitation. What feels like an attack may be a divine summons to trust deeper, stand firmer, and act bolder than ever before.

Danger removes the illusion of control. It reminds us that faith was never meant to exist only in calm waters. Faith was designed for storms. Courage is the muscle faith develops when resistance appears. Many believers pray only for deliverance from danger, but God often seeks development through it. Not every danger is meant to destroy you, some are meant to activate you. They force you to confront fear, reject passivity, and step into the strength God placed within you long before the threat appeared. When danger stands before you, heaven watches your response. Will you shrink back, or will you advance in faith? Will fear dictate your steps, or will courage rise to meet the moment? Danger does not mean God has abandoned you. Often, it means He is closer than ever calling you higher, deeper, and stronger. The very thing trying to intimidate you may be the instrument God is using to awaken your courage. Let danger do its work. Let courage awaken. And step forward not in fear, but in faith.

Courage is not the absence of fear, it's acting in the face of fear. Those who are fearful and weak don't take risks. They choose comfort and security over opportunity. A warrior, on the other hand, looks fear in the eye and spits in its face because he knows fear is not his master. Fear may roar, but faith roars louder. Fear may threaten, but truth answers back. Fear may shake the ground, but a warrior is anchored in God. A warrior understands that fear is not a sign to stop but it is often a sign that something meaningful lies ahead. Where fear tries to intimidate, faith steps forward. The warrior does not run from fear. He closes the distance. He steps toward it. He studies it. He confronts it. And when he does, fear is exposed for what it truly is - a voice without authority, a threat without power, a shadow without substance. Warriors know they have the God-given ability to overcome any obstacle that comes their way. They also know that looking fear in the eye is the beginning of victory.

Courage is often misunderstood. Many believe courage means feeling brave, fearless, or unshaken. Scripture teaches otherwise. Biblical courage is not emotional; it is obedience under pressure. It moves forward despite resistance. The warrior feels fear, his heart races, and his hands may shake. Still, his feet move forward. True courage is obedience that refuses to wait for comfort. It acts while fear screams. It obeys while doubt argues. It trusts when the path ahead is unclear. The defining mark of a warrior is not the absence of fear, but the refusal to bow to it. He moves anyway. He prays anyway. He stands anyway. The warrior's victory is not found in flawless confidence but in relentless faith. He takes the enemy's best shot and still stands strong and continues to move forward. He perseveres in the midst of all kinds of adversity and fights for what matters most. A warrior works the hardest and the longest and outlasts the competition. Having courage is the recognition of your potential.

Warriors are men of action, men who are not defined by words, intentions, or promises. The men of God were never called to sit on the sidelines, waiting for life to become easier or circumstances to improve. Warriors tackle life head-on. They face resistance, opposition, and uncertainty but they move forward anyway. A warrior understands that battles are not avoided; they are to be fought, and they are to be won. While others hesitate, the warrior steps forward. While fear whispers retreat, the warrior advances in faith. While excuses offer comfort, the warrior chooses obedience. Faith was never meant to be passive. Faith acts. Faith moves. Faith fights. Warriors do not deny the reality of hardship - they confront it. They meet adversity with courage, pressure with resolve, and conflict with conviction. They don't wait for perfect conditions; they create momentum through obedience and trust in God. Every step taken in obedience positions the warrior for victory.

Every battle faced with faith sharpens the warrior's strength. Every challenge overcome builds confidence. A warrior knows that victory does not always come without scars, but it always comes with growth. These are the men who refuse to live timid lives. They rise early, stand firm, and move boldly. They accept responsibility. They protect what matters. They fight for truth, integrity, and purpose. Warriors are men of action, men who refuse to quit, men who confront life head-on, and men who win the battles they fight because they fight with faith, discipline, and unwavering resolve. You cannot always control your circumstances, but you can control your response to your circumstances. Warriors take the initiative and do not run away from problems. On the battlefield is where he is most comfortable. Warriors have an inner supply of conquering energy and with holy boldness makes a positive impact on the world. This is not about power; it's about strength of character.

Warriors are those who "mount up with wings of eagles. They shall run and not be weary, they shall run and not faint" (Is. 40:31). Warriors fight the good fight of faith and lay hold of the eternal life which they have been called (1 Tim. 6:12). A true warrior does not fight for ego, applause, or temporary gain. He fights with a purpose rooted in noble things and eternal values. His strength is not reckless, and his courage is not impulsive. Every step he takes and every battle he faces is measured against a higher calling. He fights for what outlives him, things such as honor over comfort, truth over popularity, and obedience over convenience. While others chase momentary rewards, the warrior sets his eyes on what is eternal. He knows that what is built on pride will fall, but what is built on obedience to God will stand forever. A warrior's purpose gives meaning to his endurance. When the battle is long and the cost is high, he does not retreat, because he knows why he fights.

A warrior's strength is fueled by conviction, his endurance by hope, and his resolve by faith. He presses forward not for personal glory, but to fulfill the assignment placed upon his life. He doesn't ask whether the fight is easy, he asks whether it is worthy. Warriors don't fight for the sake of fighting. They fight when there is a reason to fight. David asked before facing Goliath, "Is there not a cause?" (1 Sam. 17:29). In that moment, David revealed the secret of true spiritual courage. He put purpose before power. David saw what others saw: a giant, a threat, an impossible situation. But he also saw what others missed: the honor of God was at stake. This was not about proving himself, gaining fame, or silencing critics. This was about defending what mattered eternally. David refused to fight merely because he was offended; he fought because there was a cause worth standing for. Warriors ask themselves, "Is this challenge about my comfort or about God's glory?"

Many soldiers were armed that day, but only one man was aligned. David's strength flowed from clarity. When the cause is clear, courage follows. When the motive is pure, faith rises. Giants lose their power when we remember why we stand. David teaches us that not every fight is worth engaging in, but every God-given cause is worth everything. When the cause is righteous, heaven backs the battle. When the cause is eternal, stones become weapons and shepherds become champions. So before you step into your next challenge, ask the question David asked. Let it search your heart. Let it steady your faith. Is there not a cause? If the answer is yes, then stand firm. God still honors those who fight for what matters most. Esther said, "And so I will go to the King, which is against the law; and if I perish, I perish" (Esther 4:16). Courage is not the absence of fear; it's the conviction that something else is more important. Courage doesn't pull back. It doesn't deny fear, it presses into fear.

Being brave doesn't mean you never get scared. It means that even when you are scared, you step up and do the things you have to do. Is. 40:29 says God "gives power to the weak, and to those who have no might He increases strength." This promise is not reserved for the strong, the confident, or the accomplished. It is spoken directly to the weary, the exhausted, and the overwhelmed. God does not wait for us to become powerful before He helps us. No, He meets us in our weakness. Weakness is not a disqualification in the kingdom of God. In fact, it is often the very doorway through which His power enters. When our strength runs out, God's strength begins. When we have "no might," He does not merely restore what was lost - He increases strength beyond what we had before. Isaiah reminds us that human strength is limited. The young grow tired and the strong stumble. But God's power is not affected by time, circumstance, or exhaustion. He never grows weary and never runs out of strength to give.

What we lack, He supplies. What we cannot carry, He carries for us. God's power flows most freely to those who know they need Him, through hearts that know they cannot stand alone. Where humility admits need, God's power finds its greatest expression. Your need becomes the doorway for God's power. When you stop striving in your own strength and turn to Him in humility, His power becomes active in your life. The weak are not ignored, they are strengthened. The empty are not dismissed, they are filled. If you feel drained, discouraged, or unable to go on, Is. 40:29 is God's reassurance to you. Your weakness has caught His attention. Your lack has invited His supply. The same God who formed the heavens stoops down to strengthen the faint. You may feel weak but, rest assured, you are not abandoned. You may feel empty, but you are not finished. God gives power to the weak, and He increases strength to those who have none. So lean into Him and man up in His strength.

Real men step beyond comfort, beyond certainty, beyond applause. They move where faith is required, where failure is possible and fear is real. They practice climbing out on the limb because that's where all the fruit is. Warriors go after it, those who are fearful cling to the trunk of the tree. And yes, sometimes the limb breaks. The fall comes hard. Pride takes a hit. Plans collapse. Confidence gets bruised. But a real man doesn't stay down rehearsing the fall or blaming the tree. He gets up, he dusts himself off, and he climbs again. God never called men to play it careful - He called them to walk by faith, not by sight. Every step of obedience carries risk. Every act of courage invites resistance. But growth only happens out on the limb. The man who never falls is the man who never tried. The man who never risks is the man who never learns the strength of God beneath him. Failure does not disqualify a man, quitting does. Courage is a choice so man up and go out on that limb.

Real men understand that the fall broken limb builds wisdom. And each time he climbs again, he gets stronger than he was before. Not because he trusts the limb but because he trusts God. Real men are not measured by how often they fall but by how often they rise, trust again, and step back out in faith. He is not defined by a flawless record. He is revealed in the moments when everything has gone wrong and he chooses to stand back up anyway. Every man falls. Even the strongest stumble. Faith does not erase failure; it redeems it. What separates real men from defeated men is not how often they fall, but how often they rise. A real man rises after the loss, after the disappointment, after the betrayal, and after the prayer that didn't seem to get answered the way he hoped. He understands that falling does not disqualify him. Quitting does. God does not measure men by their worst moments. He measures them by their willingness to get back up and keep walking with Him.

Declare war on passivity, comfort over courage. Man up! When you don't operate in courage, a part of you dies. Fear isn't your problem. Your problem is not facing your fears head on. Men are passive because they wimp out. The army of Israel feared Goliath, but David ran toward the giant. Those who are passive lack the will to do what's right. They lack courage. They think it's easier to do nothing. They think if they ignore a problem maybe it will go away. What is the solution to passivity? Man up! Do it anyway. Consider Jesus who went into Jerusalem knowing that torture and death awaited Him. Adam was passive in the garden (Gen. 3:6) but Jesus rejected passivity. A warrior does not stand around and do nothing. Jesus did something. You can too. Courage is a confidence in God's ability. Caleb said, "Let's go up at once and possess it, for we are well able to overcome it" (Num. 17:30). Courage says you can do it, fear says you can't. Who will you listen to?

| 8 |

"A GLOBAL STIRRING"

A call is going out across the earth, a global stirring that is not broadcast by media, enforced by governments, or shaped by culture. It is a divine summons that is quiet to the ears of the distracted, yet thunderous to the hearts of men who are listening. This is the call to courageous manhood. In every generation, God has called men to stand when others shrink back. He has never sought crowds of passive observers but men willing to man up, bear responsibility, and walk in obedience. Today is no different. Though the world has changed, the call remains the same, "Be strong and of good courage, do not fear nor be afraid of them; for the Lord your God, He is the One who goes with you. He will not leave you nor forsake you" (Deut. 31:6). From the bustling streets of modern cities to the remote corners of the world, men are feeling an inner unrest - a holy dissatisfaction with weakness, compromise, and spiritual drift. This is not coincidence. It is the Spirit of God stirring men awake.

Across cultures and continents, men are realizing that comfort has made them careless, and convenience has dulled their resolve. They sense that something vital has been lost and that they have been created for more. This stirring is the echo of God's call, reminding men that they were never meant to be spectators in life or in faith. Courageous manhood is being awakened because the times demand it. Families are under pressure. Truth is challenged. Moral clarity is fading. In response, God is not lowering His standard - He is raising up His men. The world's version of manhood is often loud, aggressive, and self-serving. God's version is different. Courageous manhood is not domination; it is responsibility. It is not pride; it is humility under authority. It is not the absence of fear, but the decision to act righteously despite it. A courageous man stands firm in truth even when it isolates him. He chooses obedience over popularity, integrity over convenience, and faith over fear.

He is a man who understands that strength without character is dangerous, but strength governed by righteousness is powerful. True courage is seen in repentance, in restraint, in sacrifice, and in perseverance. It is the courage to forgive, to lead, to serve, and to endure. This kind of manhood does not impress the world, but it moves heaven. Where courageous men remain silent, confusion fills the void. When men retreat from their God-given roles, disorder follows. Homes weaken. Children wander. Communities fracture. History proves that the absence of godly men creates space for darkness to advance unchecked. Passivity is not neutral - it is destructive. It is the quiet agreement with compromise. It is the slow erosion of conviction. God never called men to sit idly by while truth is challenged and righteousness is mocked. The call to courageous manhood confronts passivity head-on. It calls men to step forward, speak up, and stand firm - not with arrogance, but with unwavering faith.

Courageous manhood begins when a man accepts responsibility for his place in God's design. Fathers are called to lead their homes, not merely provide for them. Husbands are called to love sacrificially, not conditionally. Sons are called to pursue holiness early, not postpone obedience. This call is not about titles or positions; it is about the posture of the heart. A courageous man takes ownership of his influence. He understands that his choices shape others, and his faith sets a spiritual temperature for those around him. God is raising men who will stand in prayer when no one is watching, remain faithful when no one is applauding, and walk uprightly when compromise would be easier. Courageous manhood is impossible apart from faith. Human strength fades. Resolve weakens. But faith anchors a man to something eternal. It reminds him that he does not stand alone, fight alone, or endure alone. His confidence flows not from his own ability, but from his obedience to the One who called him.

This is not a call to perfection - it is a call to commitment. God is not asking you to be flawless; He is asking you to be faithful. When a man stands up in faith, families change, churches grow stronger, and generations are impacted. He is calling men who will rise again after failure, men who will submit their strength to His will, and men who will answer the call even when it disrupts their comfort and challenges their pride. The call to courageous manhood is spoken to the heart of every man who senses that God is calling him higher, deeper, and stronger. The trumpet has sounded. The moment has arrived. The question is no longer whether the call is going out because it is. The only question that remains is this, "Will you answer the call? Will you be the man God created you to be?" God did not create you to shrink back or live passively. God never designed you to live this way. He created you to stand, to lead, to protect, and to serve. He created you to man up!

Identity comes before activity. A man of God knows who he is not because of his title, income, or status, but because of his relationship with the Creator. When identity is rooted in God, direction becomes clear. When identity is confused, men drift, compromise, and lose their way. Before God ever gave Adam a wife, a home, or a family, He gave him purpose and instruction. God did not ask Adam how he felt. He entrusted him with responsibility. Manhood begins with understanding that God created men to carry weight, not avoid it. One of the greatest failures in Scripture did not come from rebellion - it came from silence. Adam was present when Eve was deceived, yet he said nothing. He watched. He listened. He remained passive. When men refuse to act, others suffer. Families lose direction, marriages weaken, children lack examples, and churches lose strength. God does not call men to sit quietly while the enemy advances. He calls them to stand watch, to guard truth, and to lead with courage.

To "man up" means rejecting passivity and stepping into responsibility even when it's uncomfortable. Modern culture teaches men to avoid responsibility. Commitment is portrayed as confinement and accountability is viewed as pressure. But in God's kingdom, responsibility is not punishment; it is honor. A man of God does not blame his upbringing, his past failures, his environment, or other people. He owns his decisions, he accepts correction, and he grows through discipline. Excuses delay growth, ownership accelerates it. When a man accepts responsibility before God, he becomes trustworthy, first in small things, then in greater ones. Biblical strength is not loud, aggressive, or impulsive. It is steady, disciplined, and submitted to God. A strong man can control his anger, resist temptation, speak truth without cruelty, and remain faithful under pressure. Jesus Christ was the strongest man who ever lived. He confronted sin, rebuked hypocrisy, endured suffering, and obeyed the Father completely.

Leadership in God's kingdom is not demanded - it is demonstrated. A man cannot lead others where he is unwilling to go himself. His life speaks long before his words ever do. Integrity, consistency, humility, and faithfulness form the foundation of godly leadership. Leadership in the kingdom of God is not measured by how many people follow you, how visible your position is, or how powerful your voice sounds. Godly leadership is measured by character. Before God ever entrusts influence, He examines the foundation beneath it. Without a solid foundation, leadership may rise quickly but it will not stand. Scripture reminds us that "no other foundation can anyone lay than that which is laid, which is Jesus Christ." (1 Cor.

3:11). To lead as Christ leads, you must build upon the same values He demonstrated: integrity, consistency, humility, and faithfulness. These are not optional virtues; they stand as the bedrock upon which godly leadership is built. They are solid, immovable, and essential to your manhood.

Integrity is the non-negotiable core to what being a man is all about. Integrity is the inward commitment to live truthfully before God and others, the alignment of belief, character, and action. It is not perfection, but it is honesty and wholeness of heart. A leader with integrity refuses to separate private life from public calling. What they preach, they practice. What they promise, they pursue. Integrity protects a leader from compromise. It guides decisions when no one else is present to offer accountability. God values integrity because He sees the heart long before He acknowledges the platform. Leadership without integrity may attract followers, but it will never earn God's approval. God has never been impressed by titles, platforms, or applause. He looks beyond what people see and examines the heart. When integrity governs the heart, trust follows naturally. People may not always agree with a leader of integrity, but they will respect them. And respect is the currency of lasting leadership.

Consistency is integrity lived out daily. It is the steady walk of obedience that continues long after excitement fades. Many leaders begin with passion, but only consistent leaders finish well. God does not look for occasional acts of righteousness; He looks for a faithful lifestyle. Occasional righteousness may satisfy the conscience, but it does not transform the character.

Anyone can act holy on Sunday, speak wisely in public, or do good when eyes are watching. But God looks deeper. He examines the private walk, the daily choices, the unseen obedience, and the quiet surrender that no one else applauds. Consistency proves that leadership is not a performance, but a calling. It is the quiet repetition of obedience, prayer, discipline, self-control, and service that shapes a leader's influence. Consistent leaders create stability. Their presence brings confidence because people know what to expect from them. Over time consistency builds trust, and trust creates authority that cannot be forced or demanded.

Humility is strength under control and is the safeguard of leadership. It keeps power from becoming pride and authority from becoming abuse. Humble leaders recognize that their position is a stewardship, not a personal achievement. They do not dominate; they serve. They do not exalt themselves; they honor the One who entrusted them. They understand that stewardship requires a heart that fears the Lord. Every role of influence is a responsibility handed down by God. Authority is not proof of greatness; it is proof of trust. God does not give leadership as a reward for pride, but as a test of faithfulness. True humility submits to God's authority before exercising authority over others. It welcomes correction, seeks wisdom, and acknowledges dependence on God. Humility does not deny strength; it submits strength to God's purpose. Jesus taught that the greatest leaders are servants. Humility allows leaders to lift others without needing recognition. It reminds them that success is God's work, not their own.

Faithfulness is loyalty that endures. It means to remain committed to God's calling regardless of circumstances. It is serving when no one applauds, persevering when progress feels slow, and trusting God when results are unseen. God places great value on faithfulness because it reveals the heart. Anyone can be passionate for a moment. Anyone can be obedient when it is convenient. But faithfulness shows who you are when the excitement fades, the rewards are delayed, and the path becomes difficult. Faithfulness is not loud. It does not demand attention. It is proven quietly over time, in consistency, obedience, and perseverance when no one is watching. Faithful leaders steward their responsibilities well, whether they are large or small. They understand that promotion comes from God, not ambition. Faithfulness is what carries leaders through seasons of testing. It anchors them when emotions waver and challenges rise. God does not require perfection, but He does require loyalty.

God is calling all men to man up and live godly lives, to fulfill their destiny and reach the summit of courageous manhood. The world today does not need men who are weak and passive, it needs strong men who are anchored in truth and submitted to God. This is a call that cannot be silenced by culture, dulled by comfort, or ignored without consequence. It is the call of God to men everywhere to rise higher. Not higher in status, wealth, or self-importance, but higher in character, conviction, and courage. God is calling men out of passivity and into purpose, out of compromise and into consecration, out of boyhood and into godly manhood. This call is not new. From the beginning, God created man with strength, responsibility, and authority. Adam was placed in the garden not merely to enjoy it, but to tend it and guard it. Before sin entered the world, before temptation came, man was already given the responsibility to watch, to protect, to lead. Courageous manhood was God's design from the start.

One of the greatest spiritual battles facing men today is not outright rebellion - it is passivity. Many men have not rejected God; they have simply drifted. They settle for spiritual minimalism, offering God leftover time, half-hearted obedience, and muted devotion. Yet Scripture never calls men to be mild, timid, or disengaged. It calls them to be strong in the Lord, vigilant, sober-minded, and ready to stand. Passivity weakens homes, erodes marriages, and leaves children without clear examples of godly leadership. When men shrink back, oftentimes the world, with its distorted definitions of masculinity, fill the void. God's answer to this crisis is not shame, but summons. He calls men higher, reminding them who they are and what they were created to be. The call of God is not merely to do more, but to be more, to become who He originally designed you to be. When God calls a man higher, He is reminding him of who he is. God's call lifts your eyes above survival and points your heart toward purpose.

You are not defined by your failures, your past mistakes, or the labels placed on you by the world. You are defined by your Creator. You were created to lead with integrity, to walk in courage, to stand firm in truth, and to live with moral and spiritual backbone. God calls men higher by awakening their identity. He reminds men that they were created in His image, that they are not weak and careless but deliberate, disciplined, and strong. Strength in God's kingdom is not arrogance or domination; it is responsibility, restraint, and resolve. It is the strength to protect what is good, to confront what is wrong, and to remain faithful when no one is watching. God calls men higher by summoning them to maturity. Boys react. Men respond. Boys avoid responsibility. Men embrace it. God calls men to grow beyond excuses and step into ownership of their faith, their character, their families, and their calling. Spiritual maturity means choosing obedience over comfort and conviction over convenience.

God calls men higher by reminding them what they were created for. You were created to walk with God, not behind Him and not ahead of Him but with Him. You were created to reflect His nature in a broken world, to bring order where there is chaos, light where there is darkness, and hope where there is despair. You were created to fight the right battles, build what matters, and leave a legacy that honors God. The call higher is a call to man up. It is a call to shake off spiritual laziness, silence the voice of fear, and reject the low expectations of the world. God is not calling men to blend in; He is calling them to stand out. Not in pride, but in purpose. Godly manhood is not measured by physical strength alone, nor by dominance or bravado. True manhood is forged in obedience, humility, and resolve. A godly man fears the Lord, not men. He chooses righteousness even when it costs him comfort or popularity. He guards his heart, disciplines his body, and submits his will to God.

Courageous manhood means standing firm when it would be easier to retreat. It means speaking truth when silence feels safer. It means leading with love, not control, and serving without seeking applause. This kind of manhood does not happen by accident - it is formed through surrender to God and daily obedience to His Word. God is calling men higher into holiness. Not a shallow, outward appearance of righteousness, but a deep, inward transformation. Holiness demands separation from the world, not isolation but distinction from its ways. A godly man does not flirt with sin or justify compromise. He understands that what he tolerates privately will eventually weaken him publicly. Holiness requires courage because it often places a man at odds with the culture around him. But God never calls a man to holiness without empowering him to walk it out. The same Spirit who raised Christ from the dead dwells within every man, strengthening them to live set-apart lives.

Biblical courage is not recklessness; it is strength under submission to God. A courageous man knows when to fight and when to kneel. He is bold in faith yet gentle in spirit. He is disciplined, not driven by impulse. He understands that true power flows from obedience to God, not from asserting control over others. Jesus Himself modeled perfect manhood. He was resolute, compassionate, fearless, and obedient to the Father even unto death. He confronted evil, protected the vulnerable, and never wavered from His mission. In Him, men see what it truly means to live courageously and godly. This call is urgent because the world desperately needs godly men who will stand in the gap, lead their families, serve their communities, and honor God with their lives. God is calling all men higher. He is calling men to live lives marked by courage, conviction, and godliness. This is the hour for men to rise, to reclaim their God-given identity, and to walk boldly in the purpose for which they were created.

| 9 |

"BORN FOR BATTLE"

Courage is not the absence of fear, but rather the judgment that something else is more important. What comes to mind when you think of courage? Many think of a lion as a symbol of strength, courage, and gallantry. In "The Wizard Of Oz" the lion is missing the one quality that should define him the most: courage. Fear crippled his ability to see himself as he actually was. As the movie unfolds, he discovered he always had courage, he just didn't show it. All men are born with the potential to show courage. Without courage you cannot practice any other virtue with consistency. You can't be kind, true, sincere, merciful, generous, or honest without courage. You also have courage. Are you displaying it? Men are often taught that courage means having no fear. That's a false teaching and it's dangerous. Fear is not weakness; surrendering to fear is. Courage is not the absence of fear. Courage is the judgment that something else matters more.

A man of God does not wait until he feels brave. He acts because he knows what is right. Courage is not an emotion; it is a decision. It is choosing obedience when fear says retreat, choosing responsibility when comfort says quit, and choosing faith when consequences look costly. God is not looking for men who never feel fear. He is looking for men who refuse to be ruled by it. Fear is natural but it must not be your master. Every man faces fear: the fear of failure, the fear of rejection, the fear of confrontation, the fear of loss, and the fear of responsibility. Fear is part of being human, but a man of God does not allow fear to sit on the throne of his life. Fear will always present reasons to hesitate. Courage evaluates those reasons and answers with obedience. A man who follows Christ learns to recognize fear without obeying it. You can feel fear and still move forward. That is strength. Fear will always suggest the easier path. Courage takes the harder road because it is the manly thing to do.

Courage shows up when a man speaks truth instead of staying silent, when a man stands firm instead of blending in, when a man protects instead of withdrawing, when a man obeys God instead of pleasing people. Courage lifts its eyes upward and asks, "What does God require of me?" Courage will cost you something. It may cost approval, popularity, or ease. But cowardice costs far more. Cowardice will cost you your spiritual authority, moral clarity, self-respect, and your impact on others. A man who avoids hard obedience slowly loses strength. A man who embraces courage even when he is afraid builds spiritual muscle. Men are not destroyed by fear. They are diminished by surrendering to it. No man suddenly becomes courageous in a crisis. Courage is forged in private obedience long before public tests appear. Courage is built when a man prays consistently, takes responsibility seriously, keeps his word, repents quickly, and obeys God when no one is watching.

Jesus is the pattern of courageous manhood. He was not weak. He was not passive. He was not fearful, yet He felt the weight of suffering. In the Garden of Gethsemane, He faced the full cost of obedience. Courage did not remove the deep struggle He was in; it carried Him through it. It was His courage that said, "Not My will, but Yours be done." Real manhood is not about dominance; it is about submission to God and strength in obedience. Real men do not wait until fear disappears. They move forward anyway. They lead when it's hard, speak when it's costly, and obey when they don't see the outcome. Fear loses power the moment a man steps forward in faith. Courage is not found in a lack of fear; it is found in a settled conviction that God is worth obeying no matter what the cost may be. All men are called to stand, to lead, to protect, to obey. You don't need to feel fearless. You need to be faithful. And every time you choose faith over fear, you become the man God is shaping you to be.

Who are you? You are a warrior, and you are called to win major battles in life. You already have courage, but you will have major challenges that you must face so that you can display courage. You were not created to live small, to hide in fear, or retreat when pressure comes. You were born for battle. From the moment God formed you, He placed something fierce inside you - a strength meant to stand, a courage meant to advance, and a faith meant to overcome. You were created to man up! You are not wandering through life by accident. You are called, and that calling includes fighting major battles. The truth be told, battles are proof of your calling. Battles do not mean you are losing. Battles mean you are needed. No one is sent to fight small wars when they are built for great victories. The size of the resistance often reveals the size of the purpose. The enemy does not waste effort on those who pose no threat. If the pressure is intense, it is because what you carry matters.

You are trained through resistance. You are facing challenges that require strength, endurance, and faith because you were designed to develop all three. A warrior is not made in comfort; he is shaped in the fire. Every trial has been sharpening you. Every setback has been training you. Every season of struggle has been building spiritual muscle. What tried to break you has actually been preparing you. God has been teaching your hands to fight and your heart to trust Him fully. You are learning how to stand when others quit and how to move forward when the way looks impossible. Weak men who are wimps don't take risks. They choose comfort and security over opportunity. Real men who man up don't run for cover. They run toward danger knowing that they have the God-given ability to overcome any obstacle that comes their way. For real men, courage isn't something they display every now and then, but rather something they showcase every moment of their lives.

Warriors eat problems for breakfast, lunch, and supper. They do it for fun. They see it as part of who they are. They look at every problem as a set of weights that will help them grow stronger. Danger is your opportunity to awaken courage. Courage sleeps quietly until its awakened by an opportunity to confront danger head-on. You were not called merely to survive battles; you were called to win them. Victory is not reserved for the strongest, the loudest, or the most confident. Victory belongs to those who refuse to surrender their faith. When you fight in obedience, courage, and humility before God, the outcome is already settled. The battle may be fierce, but the promise is sure. The fight may be long, but the victory is certain. Do not retreat and do not doubt who you are. Do not underestimate what God can do through you. Lift your head up high, set your feet, and take your place. You are a warrior, you are called to fight, and you are called to win the major battles of your life.

Webster's Dictionary defines "courage" as 'the attitude of facing and dealing with anything recognized as dangerous, difficult, or painful, instead of withdrawing from it; it's the quality of being fearless or brave; valor.' Biblical manhood is not defined by the absence of fear; it is defined by action in the presence of fear. Every man who answers God's call will face fear. Fear is not a sign that something is wrong; it is often a sign that something important is at stake. Courage is the moment a man decides that obedience to God, responsibility to others, and faithfulness to truth matter more than his personal comfort or safety. A man does not wait for fear to leave before he acts. He acts because God has spoken. He knows that men are not called to be fearless, they are called to be faithful. The world tells men to "man up" by hiding fear. Scripture tells men to stand up in spite of fear. Fear does not disqualify a man. Silence does. Faithful men do not deny fear; they refuse to be ruled by it.

Courage rises when a man decides that his duty before God outweighs his desire for safety. This is the dividing line between passive men and disciplined men. Scripture consistently connects courage to responsibility. God told Joshua to be strong and courageous because he was entrusted with leading others. David stepped toward Goliath because the honor of God and the safety of Israel mattered more than his own life. Courage shows up when a man realizes others are depending on him. A man who avoids courage avoids responsibility. A man who embraces courage becomes a covering for others. A man may endure much for himself, but something shifts when he realizes others are depending on him. When his strength is no longer optional. When his presence is no longer about preference, but purpose. In that moment, courage awakens. True courage is not born in isolation. It is forged in responsibility. This is why courage so often rises in fathers, husbands, leaders, and protectors.

A man discovers that fear can be endured when failure would leave others exposed. God designed courage to awaken through a man's calling. Scripture shows us men who stepped forward only when the weight of responsibility became clear. There were times when the flock needed a shepherd, when the people needed a voice, when the battle demanded a stand. Courage met them there not as a feeling, but as an act of obedience. A man becomes courageous when he understands that his strength is not just for him, that his faith covers others, his discipline protects others, and his perseverance secures others. And when that realization settles in his spirit, hesitation gives way to resolve. Courage is the moment a man says, "I may be afraid, but I will not abandon my post." This is the courage that God honors, the courage that rises when a man knows he is needed, the courage that stands firm because others are counting on him to stand. That is not weakness. It is manhood awakened by responsibility.

Courage is proven through the actions men do, through leading a family, standing up for truth, correcting what is wrong, making difficult decisions, and walking alone when others retreat. Fear tries to convince a man to delay, defer, or disengage. Courage refuses passivity. Courage moves forward because leadership demands action. A man becomes courageous by acting courageously especially when fear is present. Fear shrinks when a man moves forward. Fear thrives on delay and indecision. Action weakens fear's hold. Every step of obedience strengthens a man's spiritual backbone. It causes confidence to grow and faith to deepen. Over time, fear loses its authority because it has been repeatedly challenged. Men do not conquer fear by thinking about it; they conquer it by moving through it. Courage is an act of faith toward God. Courage is not recklessness; it is reverent trust. Courage says, "I trust God more than I trust my fear." That posture establishes spiritual authority in a man's life.

Courage is not the absence of fear. Courage is a man acting because God's call is greater than his fear. Do not wait until fear disappears. It may never fully leave. Instead, decide what matters more. Choose obedience over comfort, choose responsibility over retreat, choose faith over fear. Courage is not the absence of fear. Courage is a man acting because God's call is greater than his fear. Courage is not reserved for extraordinary moments. It is forged in daily obedience, by choosing integrity when compromise is easier, loving when bitterness feels justified, leading when retreat feels safer, persevering when the path is difficult. Men who practice courage in small decisions are prepared when great tests come. 1 Sam. 17 tells the story of David and Goliath. David was a fearless warrior. What helped him display his courage? Practice! Practice! Practice! David practiced courage before he faced Goliath. He killed the lion and the bear before he killed the giant.

David worked his way up the ladder of courage. You must climb the little mountain before you climb the big one. Michael Jordan once said, "I have missed more than 9,000 shots in my career. I have lost almost 300 games. On 26 occasions I have entrusted to take the game-winning shot and missed. I've failed over and over and over again in my life. And that is why I succeed." No one ever becomes a success in life without first having had multiple failures. But if you practice enough, when reality strikes, you'll be ready for it. Become numb to failure. Courage is a maximum-gain strategy. Most men are not defeated by sin; they are defeated by discouragement. They stop moving, stop speaking, stop risking, not because God has withdrawn His call, but because they fear falling again. This is why they walk away from their dream. Michael Jordan, Abraham Lincoln, Thomas Edison, and Colonel

Sanders all had multiple failures in their quest to accomplish a great work. Would anybody call these men failures?

God is not looking for men who never fail. He is looking for men who refuse to quit. To become numb to failure is not to grow cold - it is to grow strong. It is to lose sensitivity to shame while gaining sensitivity to the voice of God. It is to stop flinching every time something goes wrong and to keep advancing even when the outcome is uncertain. Failure feels final only when identity is weak. When a man doesn't know who he is, every mistake feels like a verdict. But when identity is rooted in God, failure becomes instruction, not condemnation. The Bible is filled with men who failed loudly, publicly, and repeatedly yet they were still chosen, still anointed, still used. Moses doubted and disobeyed before he led a nation. David collapsed morally after rising spiritually. Peter denied Jesus at the moment courage mattered most. Yet God did not remove their calling. He refined their character. Failure did not cancel God's plan, but fear would have. Satan only needs you to stay down once you've fallen.

Every act of obedience carries risk. Every calling requires courage. Every step of faith involves the possibility of failure. The men God used most were not those who avoided mistakes, but those who refused to let mistakes silence them. Courage is not the absence of fear—it is obedience in spite of it. Faith initiates the vision, but courage executes it. Without courage, faith remains theoretical. This is why courage is a maximum-gain strategy. Courage accelerates growth, attracts God's strength, and exposes fear and strips it of its power. When a man chooses courage, he gains something far greater than success. He gains spiritual authority. The kingdom of God does not advance through careful calculation. It advances through men who step forward while the outcome is still unknown. A man who has failed and risen carries depth. He carries compassion. He carries credibility. He no longer boasts in perfection; he boasts in . Failure becomes dangerous only when it leads to retreat.

All men who man up become numb to failure. They stop replaying past defeats, stop requiring perfect conditions before they move, stop waiting for confidence before acting, and they stop allowing embarrassment to dictate their obedience. They move forward bruised but unbroken, corrected but committed, humbled but undeterred. This is spiritual toughness. A man numb to failure cannot be controlled by criticism, intimidated by resistance, or silenced by setbacks. He listens to God instead of always playing it safe. Playing it safe feels responsible, but it slowly kills purpose. Comfort is expensive. It costs vision, growth, and legacy. The greatest regret will never be, "I tried and failed." It will be, "I was called but never moved." God does not reward passivity. He rewards faith expressed through courage. Do not ask God to remove failure from your path. Ask Him to remove fear from your heart because in the kingdom of God, courage is the strategy that produces maximum gain.

David used his connection to an infinite God to overshadow the fear of what he saw and what he heard. Goliath had better equipment and was physically superior in size and strength.

David's only defense was God, and that was enough. God is infinite and more powerful. What or who can stand up to that? Having God on your side is a confidence booster that allows you to display more courage. Courage is having radical obedience in the face of what scares you the most. It's not pulling back. It's pressing forward into your fears, not denying your fears. It's about seeing what needs to be advanced and what needs to be accomplished as being greater than your personal comfort. Real men man up and explore their spiritual nature. They look to God for guidance and strength because with Him on your side you can take on anything! A real man doesn't run away. When you don't operate in courage, a part of you dies. Every action that you take that lacks courage is like cutting yourself with a knife.

The greatest rewards in life are typically preceded by some of life's greatest challenges. Wimps discover the "cost factor" and are so focused on the cost that they can't see the reward. Fear in and of itself isn't their problem. Their problem is not facing their fear head-on. What's the solution? Man up! Do it anyway! If you have to, do it afraid! You have to learn to do what you have to do, even if you're afraid to do it. For real men, life isn't about getting comfortable where they're at right now. Wimps have retirement on their mind and a comfortable life as their goal. For a real man, life is all about breaking barriers and going to the next level. Manhood is a continuous journey that requires you to stay in motion. That takes courage. Courage is spitting in the face of your fear by taking action. When you're scared and you want to draw back, that is exactly the time you should go faster, move forward, and do more. Fear runs much faster than courage, yet it never has enough energy to finish the race.

| 10 |

"STIFF SPINES"

Most men don't know what courage is just like they don't know what authentic manhood is. Sometimes men have to do things they're afraid to do. Being brave doesn't mean you never get scared, it means that even when you are scared you step up and do the things men have to do. Courage is a choice so choose to be brave. Make your life count because strong men are forged when one man chooses courage. Billy Graham once said, "Courage is contagious. When one brave man takes a stand, the spines of others are stiffened." All men need to man up and stand strong with stiff spines. Courage rarely announces itself with noise. More often, it shows up quietly like when one man decides he will not bend, will not retreat, will not stay silent when truth is at stake. Yet something remarkable happens in that moment: courage spreads. When one brave man takes a stand, others discover strength they didn't know they had. Fear loses its grip and what once felt impossible suddenly feels necessary.

God has always worked this way. He looks for one heart willing to trust Him, one voice willing to speak, one life willing to obey. That single act of faith becomes a spark. And sparks ignite fires. History and Scripture are filled with moments where one man's courage awakened many. One man refused to bow, and a nation saw the power of God. One man stepped onto the battlefield, and an army found its backbone. One man stood before injustice, and others found the strength to follow. Courage is never meant to be hoarded. It's meant to be modeled. When you stand firm, you give silent permission for others to do the same. When you refuse to back down, others will rise up and stand with you. Your obedience strengthens their resolve. Your faith stiffens their spine. This is why the enemy works so hard to isolate, intimidate, and silence men of conviction. He knows that if he can stop one, he may stop many. But if one man stands - truly stands - the ripple effect cannot be contained.

You may not see who is watching and you may not realize who is drawing strength from your decision. But someone is. Your courage matters more than you think so man up because when one brave man takes a stand, courage multiplies and God moves. Courage does not begin with a crowd. It begins with a man. Every great movement of God starts the same way - not with mass agreement, but with a single heart that decides, "I will stand, even if I have to stand alone." Before armies move, before cultures shift, before families change, one man draws a line and refuses to step back. That is how courage works. It is personal before it becomes powerful. Most men are not waiting for a speech. They are waiting for an example to follow. They are watching to see if anyone will stand when it costs something. And when one man finally does, something awakens in the hearts of others. Fear begins to lose its authority, excuses begin to sound hollow, and conviction begins to rise. Courage is contagious.

Every man knows what he should do. The real battle is whether he will actually do it. Men hesitate because standing alone feels dangerous. It invites criticism. It threatens comfort. It exposes weakness. The enemy whispers lie after lie in his ear, saying, "It's not worth it. You'll look foolish. Just stay quiet." Silence feels safer than resistance. Blending in feels easier than standing out. But neutrality has never been strength - it is simply delayed surrender. The moment a man chooses comfort over conviction, he teaches others to do the same. But the opposite is also true: the moment a man chooses courage; he gives permission for others to rise. That's the ripple effect of courage. One brave man never stands alone for long. When one man speaks truth, another finds his voice. When one man resists compromise, another gains resolve. When one man refuses to bow, when he man's up, others straighten their backs. Courage releases courage. Faith awakens faith. Obedience stirs obedience.

Your stand is never isolated; it is multiplied. This is why Scripture so often focuses on individuals. God does not wait for the majority; He moves through the willing. One man stood before a giant, and an army remembered who they were. One man refused to bow, and a nation saw the power of God. One man obeyed when obedience was costly, and generations were changed. The enemy fears courageous men more than talented ones. A skilled man can be distracted. A gifted man can be corrupted. But a courageous man - rooted in truth and obedience - is dangerous. That is why the enemy isolates men, convinces them they are alone, and magnifies the cost of obedience while minimizing its impact. He wants men to believe their stand won't matter. But heaven sees differently. God watches for the man who will stand before the breakthrough, before the applause, before the reinforcement arrives. A man aligned with God is surrounded at all times, even when he stands by himself.

True courage is revealed when no one is clapping. It's easy to stand when the crowd agrees with you all the time. It's harder when obedience is quiet, private, and unseen. Yet this is where God forges warriors. Men who stand in private strengthen the foundation for public victory. Long before a man leads others, he must lead himself. Every battle tests more than strength - it tests conviction. When the noise of the crowd fades, when encouragement is silent, and when the fight becomes personal, the question is simple, "Can you stand when no one else is standing with you?" A man who cannot stand alone will not stand long in battle, because battles are rarely won in moments of applause. They are won in moments of resolve when fear presses in, fatigue weighs heavy, and retreat feels like the reasonable thing to do. Standing alone does not mean standing without God. It means standing without depending on the approval of others, without needing permission from the crowd to do what is right.

Scripture is filled with men who stood alone before they ever stood victorious. David stood alone when others trembled at

Goliath. Daniel stood alone when obedience meant a lion's den. Elijah stood alone on Mount Carmel while false prophets shouted louder than truth. Jesus stood alone in Gethsemane while His closest friends slept. Victory always begins in solitude. A man who cannot stand alone will follow the crowd into compromise, retreat at the first sign of resistance, and surrender ground God never told him to give up. But a man anchored in God's Word can stand in silence, withstand pressure, and remain immovable when everything around him shakes. Standing alone requires spiritual backbone, a settled heart that says, "Even if no one goes with me, I will obey God." That kind of man may stand alone for a season, but he will never stand weak. Heaven stands with him. And here is the truth the enemy hates most: Men who can stand alone become men others can stand behind.

When the battle intensifies - and it will - those who learned to stand in private will still be standing in public. They will not be carried by momentum or protected by numbers. They will be sustained by conviction. Stand alone now so you can stand strong when the battle comes. Because a man who learns to stand with God - even when he stands by himself - will stand to the very end. When you stand, others borrow your courage until theirs grows strong enough to stand on its own. This is how God builds men - shoulder to shoulder, strength transferred through example. Your obedience today may become another man's breakthrough tomorrow. God is not looking for perfect men, He is looking for men who will stand when it's uncomfortable, when it's unpopular, and when it's costly. Courage does not eliminate fear; it overrules it. And when one brave man takes a stand, the spines of others are stiffened, the hearts of others are strengthened, and the kingdom of God advances.

Stu Weber said, "Courage is doing the right thing in every circumstance regardless of the cost." Courage is staying with your wife when it's difficult to do so. Not all marriages are made in heaven. Courage is pulling into your driveway after a hard day on the job and knowing your work isn't done yet. Courage runs from passive behavior. You need courage to stop watching the championship ball game in order to get up and discipline your child who just disrespected your wife. Courage is the willingness to do what you have to do when you don't want to do it. Courage is needed the most and counted on the most when you are the most afraid. There will be times in your life when you will be confronted by Goliath and fear will grip your heart and try to stop you from standing up to him. Call it fear, anxiety, concern, or hesitation, the fact is that we all face moments when fear tries to keep us from something better. What should you do? Man up and do it afraid! If you don't, the good life will pass you by.

Josh. 1:9 says, "Be strong and of good courage; Be not afraid, neither be dismayed, for the Lord thy God is with thee wherever you go." If you will move forward and do it afraid, you will find that fear loses its grip. Faith is confidence in God's ability that says "you can do it" while fear says you can't. Phil. 4:13 says, "You can do all things through Christ that strengthens you." Moses sent 12 spies into the Promised Land. Ten spies said, "We are not able to go up against the people, for they are stronger than we are" (Num. 13:31,32). Caleb with Joshua said, "Let us go up at once and possess it, for we are well able to overcome it" (Num. 13:30). One of the favorite sayings of Jesus was, "Fear not" (Luke 8:50; Luke 12:32). 2 Tim. 1:7, "For God has not given us a spirit of fear, but of power and of love and of a sound mind." The problem is too many men make the devil out to be bigger than he actually is. They give him way too much credit and, by listening to them talk, you would think he was bigger than God.

These men don't seem to realize we will one day gaze upon the devil and ask, "Is this the man who made the earth tremble, who shook nations?" (Is.14:16). Still, they make him out to be the Mike Tyson of the spiritual underworld. Mike Tyson was the ultimate warrior. He was young, relentless, forceful, and solid through and through. He was a modern-day Goliath and so awesome was the destruction of his opponents that knees trembled at the mention of his name. He fought with the ferociousness of a rabid pit-bull and easily was able to force his will on those in front of him. Mike Tyson was the school yard bully who no one would stand up to. Fear and intimidation caused his opponents to lose the fight before they even stepped into the ring with him. Mike Tyson was sitting on top of the world until one day the unthinkable happened. Like the real Goliath, he also got confronted by a fighter who was unwilling to back down, a man immovable under pressure, a man steadfast in the face of opposition.

A no-name fighter named Buster Douglas was picked to be Mike Tyson's next victim. He was a man who refused to submit his will to that of Mike Tyson for he had found a weak link in the champion's armor. It seems that Mike Tyson did not respond well when he himself was hit with a hard punch. Instead of continuing his relentless forward onslaught, he would stop for a second, step back, collect himself, and then continue on. This slight moment of hesitation was all Buster Douglas needed. He knew if you wanted to beat Mike Tyson you had to take the fight to him. You had to confront this man who fought like a raging bull. Buster Douglas had to suck up the pain and, during this moment of hesitation, had to hit Mike Tyson hard over and over again. Bam! Bam! This Buster Douglas did to perfection and when the fight ended it was Mike Tyson on the floor taking the ten-count. Mike Tyson never regained the form he had before and would later get beat up and knocked out several more times.

Mike Tyson was only a shadow of the fighter he had once been, and this was all because he got confronted. To fight your spiritual battles, you will need a stiff spine, the tenacity of a Buster Douglas, and a willingness to go on the offensive and take the fight to the devil. You need to man up and confront him and the Goliaths he puts in front of you. The Bible is a book about confrontations between good and evil. It tells of confrontations that took place and, unfortunately, ones that did not. We read where a young shepherd boy named David confronted Goliath whereas Adam stood by and did not confront the serpent. We read where Elijah boldly confronted the prophets of Baal on Mt. Carmel but ran away when threatened by Jezebel. Joshua and Caleb wanted to confront the giants in the Promised Land, the others did not. With sword in hand Peter confronted those who came to arrest Jesus but not long after refused to confront those who accused him of being a disciple of Jesus.

Know with certainty that the enemy will not stop until he is confronted and refusing to do so has serious consequences. There is a dangerous lie quietly tolerated among men of weak faith. They say, "If I ignore the enemy long enough, he will eventually leave me alone." Nothing could be further from the truth. Scripture, history, and experience all agree on one unyielding reality - the enemy does not retreat out of mercy, boredom, or fatigue. He retreats only when confronted and resisted. Until then, he advances. The enemy you face - whether temptation, deception, fear, sin, or spiritual opposition - is not passive. He is not neutral. He is not waiting to see what you decide. Jesus made this unmistakably clear when He said in John 10:10, "The thief does not come except to steal, and to kill, and to destroy." He said the thief comes with persistence and the intention to take you down. An enemy who comes to destroy will not stop because you are silent. Silence is not neutrality in warfare. Silence is surrender.

Many men confuse avoidance with wisdom. They step back from confrontation, hoping to preserve peace, protect relationships, or maintain emotional comfort. But the peace purchased by avoidance is always temporary and always costly. When Adam remained silent in the garden, sin did not pause. When Israel ignored the Philistines, the giant did not shrink. When Saul spared what God commanded him to destroy, the consequences followed him for the rest of his

life. What you refuse to confront today will return tomorrow stronger, bolder, and more demanding because the enemy
interprets your refusal to act as permission to advance. One of
the enemy's greatest strategies is not immediate destruction,
but gradual erosion. Delay gives strongholds time to for-
tify. What begins as a thought becomes a habit. What begins
as a habit becomes a stronghold. What begins as a stronghold
eventually becomes bondage. The longer confrontation is
postponed, the higher the price of victory becomes.

Men who man up know that confrontation is a biblical mandate. God does not call men to passive survival - He calls them
to active resistance. James 4:7 says, "Submit yourselves therefore to God. Resist the devil, and he will flee from you." Notice
that the enemy flees after resistance, not before it. There is no
verse that says, "Ignore the devil and he will get tired." There
is no promise that says, "Avoid confrontation and victory will
come." Victory is released through obedience, courage, and action. Gal. 5:1 (MSG) says, "Christ has set us free to live a free
life. So take your stand! Never again let anyone put a harness
of slavery on you." In other words, man up and don't let Goliath push you around. The word "Goliath" means 'to strip as
in shame, disgrace, to lead into captivity.' The word "Philistine" means 'to roll in the dust' or 'wallow in the mud.' The
devil pounces on the weak, the helpless, the intimidated, those
who are afraid to stand up and confront him. Take your stand!
Man up!

All men all called to be a modern-day David with the courage
to confront Goliath. Solomon makes it clear that there is a time

in our lives for confrontation. Eccl. 3:3, "There is a time to kill, and a time to heal." Vs. 7,8 says there is "a time to tear, and a time to sew; a time to keep silence, and a time to speak; a time to love, and a time to hate; a time of war, and a time of peace." We are soldiers in the army of the Lord, and we must be forever ready to stand up and confront those forces who compromise the will of God on planet earth. Remember, a bully is a Goliath who's never been confronted, and he won't stop harassing you until he is. Spirit-led anger is the stone you put in your sling when you confront Goliath. Solomon says there is "a time for war" and you can't go to war until you first get angry. Anger is the strongest of all passions and when controlled can be used for your benefit. Anger is not sin if it's justified. Many times, Jesus got angry as did the Heavenly Father (Mark 3:5; 2 Chron. 28:25).

There are times when we are commanded by God to also get angry. Eph. 4:26 (MSG) says, "Go ahead and be angry. You do well to be angry but don't use your anger as fuel for revenge. And don't stay angry." Spirit-led anger is a method of letting the enemy know you're serious. When controlled, righteous anger is in fact God's anger manifested through you. The closer you are to God, the angrier you'll become when His will is compromised. David was a man after God's own heart and you can hear the anger in his voice when he said, "Who is this uncircumcised Philistine that he should defy the armies of the living God?" God has given us this tool of spirit-led anger in order to take a stand against sin and injustice. To defeat the enemy, you must confront him and make him more miserable than he's making you. You do that with a controlled, spirit-led anger. Do not wait or hesitate when Goliath stands in your path. Take a stand and say something. Better yet, run toward your giant and do something.

| 11 |

"A FEW GOOD MEN"

Courage is not the absence of fear, but rather the judgment that something else in more important. Courage is born at the crossroads of fear and conviction. It rises when obedience outweighs comfort, when truth outweighs safety, and when faith outweighs self-preservation. Courage says, "I am afraid, but I will act anyway because God, truth, love, and purpose demand it." Joshua stood on the edge of the Promised Land knowing battles lay ahead. Esther approached the king aware that death was a real possibility. Jesus Himself, in Gethsemane, felt the crushing weight of what was coming. Yet they moved forward. Why? Because something mattered more than their fear. Plato said, "Courage is knowing what to fear and what not to fear." Courage is a by-product of the fear of the Lord. If God says to do it, you do it. Oral Roberts once said his greatest fear was that he might not obey God. Courage says, "It's not about me. It's all about Him." It takes courage to act on biblical convictions.

A warrior is not a man who feels no fear. A warrior is a man who refuses to let fear decide his actions. A truth all men need to grasp onto is that fear is not the enemy of courage. Cowardice is. A man becomes courageous the moment he decides that fear will no longer be the highest authority in his life. Courage is the judgment that something else is more important than fear. Courage says God's calling matters more than your comfort, truth matters more than approval, obedience matters more than safety, and faith matters more than fear. A man becomes courageous the moment he decides that fear will no longer be the highest authority in his life. David didn't face Goliath because he lacked fear. He faced him because the honor of God mattered more. Joshua didn't enter the Promised Land without fear. God repeatedly told him, "Be strong and courageous," because fear would be present, but obedience was required anyway. Gideon was afraid. God didn't shame him; He strengthened him.

If fear disqualified a man from courage, there would be no heroes in scripture. A warrior understands that pain endured in obedience is always better than comfort purchased with compromise. He also understands that courage can be very expensive. It can cost you popularity, comfort, control, ease, and sometimes even relationships. That is why so few choose it. But the cost of cowardice is far greater. Cowardice slowly erodes a man's soul. It leaves him living beneath his calling, haunted by regret, knowing he settled when he was created to stand. Fear was never meant to rule you. It can inform you, but you must never let it command you. Faith puts fear in its proper place. Faith does not deny fear; it limits fear's authority in your life. Fear may knock at the door, but courage decides whether it enters. A man walking with God says, "I feel fear, but I will move anyway. I am uncertain but I will obey. I am uncomfortable, but I will man up and stand firm." That is spiritual strength. That is what it means to be a man.

Courage is not only for dramatic moments but is forged in daily decisions. It takes courage to lead your family spiritually, to admit weakness and seek accountability, and to repent and change the direction of your life. Courage is also needed to speak truth in love, walk away from sin, persevere when results are slow, and to stand firm when culture pushes back. These quiet battles shape a man more than public victories ever will. One courageous man changes more than his own life. Courage stiffens the spines of other men. When one man stands, others find the strength to follow. Courage is contagious. It creates momentum. It builds legacy. Your courage today becomes permission for another man tomorrow. Your stand becomes another man's breakthrough. Your obedience becomes another man's example. Always remember that true courage is not the absence of fear, but the judgment that something else - God's calling, God's truth, and God's purpose - is more important.

Real men are trained to think in terms of strength, responsibility, and mission. They learn early that nothing is handed to them on a silver platter and that if something matters, they must fight for it. But here is a truth many men struggle to believe - before they were ever born and before they ever fought a battle, God was already thinking about them. And this includes you. God has you on His mind and He has a plan for your life. Jer. 1:5, "Before I formed you in the womb I knew you; before you were born, I sanctified you; and I ordained you a prophet to the nations." Jer. 29:11, "For I know the thoughts that I think toward you, says the Lord, thoughts of peace and not of evil, to give you a future and a hope." The Amplified Bible says God wants "to give you hope in your final outcome." This is why you need to man up and accept by faith and with courage that God has a glorious, good plan for your life. You were not born into this world by accident. You were not shaped by chance or circumstance alone.

You were intentionally formed, placed in this generation, in this time, with this wiring, because God had you on His mind long before you ever had Him on yours. All men have been called to serve God. They've all been given an assignment from on high. They've all got a reason to live. Still, excuses abound as to why these individual calls are not fulfilled. Gideon said, "O, my Lord, how can I save Israel? Indeed, my clan is the weakest in Manasseh, and I am the least in my father's house" (Judges 6:15). Gideon was indeed flawed but for some reason he did not grasp what the Angel of the Lord said to him in vs. 12, "The Lord is with you, you mighty man of valor." Consider what Moses said to God at the burning bush, "Who am I that I should go to Pharaoh, and that I should bring the children of Israel out of Egypt?" (Ex. 3:11). God makes champions out of failures. He will take a person who is flawed and make them mighty. He'll give you beauty for ashes (Is. 61:3). He'll turn a nobody into a somebody.

God can use anybody and that includes you! You are not too old to serve God. Moses was 80 when called to deliver God's people out of Egypt. Neither are you too young. Jesus fed the multitude with the loaves and fishes of a young boy. God used murderers, adulterers, prostitutes, and smelly fishermen to do His work. Consider the lustful Samson and the ever-impulsive Peter. Who was more flawed than they? Saul of Tarsus, Moses, Gideon, Elijah, and David all made mistakes, but God used them in a mighty way. They were all flawed but mighty. God uses nobodies, people who are flawed. Read 1 Cor. 1:26-29. The New Berkley translation says, "God has chosen the world's insignificant, and despised, and nobodies, in order to bring to nothing those who amount to something so that nobody may boast in the presence of God." People who are important in their own eyes are in for a letdown when they want to be used by God. Why? Because God uses people who do not think too highly of themselves.

When God finds a somebody, He first turns them into a nobody. Not to diminish them but to prepare them. Before God can use a life publicly, He works on the heart privately. Before He entrusts influence, He removes self-importance. Before He builds the platform, He digs the foundation. Moses was raised as the son of Pharaoh's daughter but before he could be used by God he was sent to the backside of the desert for 40 years. Paul was a somebody but after being struck down on the road to Damascus he was sent to Arabia for several years away from the view of all the people. When chased by Jezebel self-pity overcame Elijah and he said, "I alone am left." In other words, "God, no one is serving You except me! What will you do without me?" Elijah became too important in his own eyes and, because he wouldn't stop complaining, God decided to replace him with a nobody farmer named Elisha. The rich young ruler was a somebody who turned his back on Jesus when he was told to become a nobody.

Faithfulness is the key to being used mightily by God (1 Cor. 4:2). You can teach a person skills to make them qualified, but you can never teach faithfulness. You are either faithful or you're not. God is not looking for qualifications or a person with great skills in a certain area. Above all else, He is looking for faithfulness. Jesus said, "He who is faithful in what is least is faithful also in much" (Luke 16:10). God always calls those who are doing something. Elisha was plowing a field, Gideon was thrashing wheat, David was taking care of his father's sheep, and Peter was fishing when the Lord called and spoke to them of their upcoming ministries. Begin to do faithfully whatever it is your hand finds to do. Men need to stop making excuses for why they're not serving the Lord. Too many men are waiting for God to do something when, in fact, it is He who is waiting on them to do something. Stop telling God how flawed and unworthy you are and begin to put your hand to the plow and do the job that is available to you.

God does not look for the many, He looks for the few. He is looking for a few good men. Always remember, the door of tomorrow will not open until you man up and do something today. David did not become king by talking about Goliath. He picked up a stone that day. Nehemiah did not rebuild the wall by dreaming. He picked up tools that day. Joshua did not see victory by hesitation. He stepped forward that day. There are doors God has already prepared for you, but they are sealed until you take responsibility for what is in front of you today. God honors action. If you won't confront what you tolerate today, you will never possess what God promised tomorrow. Manhood is not proven by what you plan to do someday. Manhood is revealed by what you do now. Heaven responds to men who rise, stand, and act. When you take responsibility today, when you obey, God opens doors no man can shut. The door of tomorrow is already there but it will not open until you move today.

A warrior does not appear on the battlefield by coincidence. He is trained, positioned, and sent. In the same way, God does not raise men without purpose. Every man He creates is placed on assignment whether he recognizes it yet or not. Before you ever faced resistance, God already saw victory. Before you ever doubted yourself, God already knew what was inside of you. While you were still trying to find your footing, He was mapping your path. The world tells men they are only as good as their last win or loss. God tells a different story. He says your value was established before the fight ever began. Your worth is not tied to your performance; it is anchored in His purpose. God's thoughts toward you are not casual. They are strategic. He thinks like a commander preparing a soldier for deployment. He sees where you've been, where you are, and where you must go. He knows what must be forged in you before you can carry what He plans to place in your hands.

God does not improvise with men's lives. He plans them. Every season of pressure, every stretch of waiting, every closed door that frustrated you all served a purpose. A warrior is not trained in comfort. He is shaped in resistance. Muscles are built under strain. Character is formed under weight. Faith is tested in the dark. What you thought was a setback was often a setup. What felt like delay was often development. God was strengthening your core, sharpening your discernment, and toughening your resolve. He was preparing you for battles you hadn't even seen yet. Many men abandon the plan because they mistake preparation for punishment. But God does not waste pain. He refines through it. Every warrior has scars. Every man of God has moments he wishes he could erase. But know with certainty that your mistakes did not cancel God's plan. God knew your failures before He called you and He called you anyway. He saw something in you that He could use for His glory.

When a soldier stumbles, a good commander doesn't throw him away. He restores him, retrains him, and sends him back stronger. God does the same. Redemption is not weakness; it is part of the strategy. Some of the most effective men in the kingdom are not the ones who never fell but are the ones who learned how to get back up, repent, realign, and move forward with humility and strength. There will be nights when you wonder if your life is making a difference. When your prayers feel unheard. When the weight of responsibility feels heavier than your strength. In those moments, remember that God has you on His mind and you matter more than you think. That means your life has meaning. That means your presence matters. That means your obedience counts even when no one sees it. Warriors do not always fight in front of crowds. Many of the most important battles are fought in private against fear, compromise, doubt, and discouragement. God sees every one of them.

Stand where you are and go forward when He says to move. A disciplined warrior knows when to stand his ground and when to advance. Trusting God does not mean passivity. It means readiness. A disciplined warrior understands that victory is not found in constant motion, nor in stubborn resistance, but in discernment. Battles are not won merely by strength or zeal, but by obedience to the right command at the right moment. In the kingdom of God, knowing when to stand is just as important as knowing when to move forward. Many men lose ground not because they lack courage, but because they lack wisdom. They fight the wrong battles, retreat when they should stand, or stand still when God is calling them to advance. Spiritual maturity is revealed in a man who can discern the season and respond accordingly. To stand means to hold the line when pressure demands compromise. It means refusing to retreat when fear, temptation, or opposition seeks to push you backward.

Standing requires discipline of the inner man. Anyone can run. Anyone can react. But it takes a trained warrior to remain unmoved when the enemy applies pressure. Standing often looks quiet, unseen, and uncelebrated but it is one of the greatest acts of faith. When God commands a man to stand, He is calling him to guard something sacred - his integrity, his calling, his family, his faith, and his obedience. To stand is to say, "I will not surrender what God has entrusted to me." It is the refusal to give ground to sin, fear, culture, or compromise. Many battles are lost not in dramatic moments, but in subtle retreats, in small concessions that slowly erode a man's strength. The disciplined warrior recognizes these moments and plants his feet firmly in truth. Standing is not passive waiting; it is active resistance. It is spiritual alertness. It is readiness. It is faith that holds fast in the waiting even when nothing appears to be happening. Faith refuses to retreat, even when there is no sign of change.

While some seasons demand stillness, others demand movement. Advancement is not recklessness; it is obedience in motion. When God says advance, hesitation becomes disobedience. Advancing requires courage because it always involves risk. It pulls a man out of comfort and into unfamiliar territory. It demands faith that God will make a way where none is visible. The advancing warrior has a deep understands that obedience sometimes means stepping forward before clarity arrives. He trusts that God reveals the path as the steps are taken, not before. Advancement is required when God is calling you into growth, when old ground has become familiar but unfruitful, when delay has turned into disobedience, and when opportunity is knocking and fear is resisting. A disciplined warrior does not advance for glory or ego. He advances because God has spoken. He moves forward with purpose and confidence. His steps are purposeful as he presses forward with clarity and resolve.

An undisciplined warrior charges forward blindly and is quickly defeated. He mistakes aggression for courage and noise for power. He fights battles God never assigned and wonders why he is weary and wounded. On the other hand, a fearful warrior refuses to move at all. He clings to comfort; resists change and calls stagnation "contentment." Over time, he does not merely stay still; he loses ground. The disciplined warrior avoids both extremes. He listens before he acts. He seeks God before he moves. He understands that every battle does not require the same response. Wisdom is knowing there is a difference between battles to endure and battles to pursue, a moment to defend and a moment to conquer, a season of holding and a season of advancing. Discernment is the battlefield skill that separates survivors from victors. Standing and advancing are not opposites - they are partners in victory. Standing protects what is holy. Advancing possesses what is promised.

A man who never stands will lose what he has. A man who never advances will never gain what God has prepared. The disciplined warrior learns to do both well. He does not rush ahead of God, nor does he lag behind Him. He moves when God moves. He holds when God commands him to hold. This kind of discipline is not learned overnight. It is forged through prayer, obedience, failure, correction, and perseverance. Over time, the warrior becomes sensitive to the voice of God and confident in His leading. In the end, victory is not determined by whether a man stands or advances; it is determined by whether he obeys. Sometimes obedience looks like immovable resolve and sometimes it looks like bold forward motion. The disciplined warrior understands that God goes before those who obey Him. When a man stands at God's command, he stands in divine strength. When a man advances at God's command, he advances under divine covering. The warrior's confidence is never in his own power, his own experience, or his own strategy. It is in but in the God who leads him. Stand when God says stand and advance when God says advance for victory always follows obedience.

| 12 |

"TAKE YOUR PLACE"

It is time to make a quality decision to step forward and do that which you were born to do. Every warrior faces a moment when talk ends and action begins. It is the moment when standing still becomes more dangerous than moving forward. In that moment, neutrality is no longer an option. You either advance or retreat but you do not remain the same. Too many men live their lives circling the battlefield instead of stepping onto it. They know God has called them to more, but they postpone obedience, telling themselves they will move when they feel ready, when conditions improve, or when fear finally loosens its grip. But warriors are not made by comfort. They are formed by decision. A quality decision is when you draw a line in the sand. Once it is drawn, there is no negotiation with fear, no debate with doubt, and no retreat to old habits. A warrior does not wait for confidence to show up. He man's up and moves forwards knowing that confidence follows in his footsteps.

God does not create men to merely survive; He creates them to lead, protect, build, and fight for what matters. There is a calling on your life that existed before you were aware of it, and it has not expired simply because you delayed responding to it. Deep inside every man is the awareness that he was made for responsibility. It shows up as restlessness when life becomes too small, too safe, or too predictable. That restlessness is not a flaw - it is a signal. It is the warrior inside you demanding that you step forward and take your place. The enemy understands this, which is why he works tirelessly to keep men distracted, discouraged, and divided against themselves. A man who never decides to man up and fulfill his heavenly call never becomes dangerous to darkness. What the enemy fears most is a man who knows why he exists and refuses to be moved away from his calling. A man who fully commits to God's purpose becomes visible, disruptive, and a threat the enemy cannot ignore.

When a man surrenders fully to God, he stops fighting random battles and steps into assigned territory. The enemy cannot ignore a man who prays with conviction, obeys without delay, and stands when retreat would be easier. Such a man disrupts plans, breaks cycles, and reclaims ground that was never meant to be lost. A man committed to God's purpose understands that opposition is confirmation, not condemnation. He recognizes resistance as evidence that his life is moving in the right direction. He does not retreat when challenged - he tightens his grip on truth and moves forward with greater resolve. This kind of man is not seeking attention, but his obedience echoes loudly in the spiritual realm. He becomes a leader whether he seeks the title or not. His presence changes atmospheres. His faith builds a foundation for others to stand on. His courage awakens dormant strength in those around him. When one man stands, others find the courage to stand with him.

The enemy knows this. That is why compromise is always offered before commitment. That is why comfort is dangled before calling. That is why fear whispers before faith speaks. But the man who commits fully to God understands that neutrality is not an option. You are either advancing God's purpose or yielding ground to the enemy. A man surrendered to God becomes a weapon in God's hand - sharpened, disciplined, and directed. He does not fight for applause. He fights for obedience. He does not chase comfort. He pursues his calling. The man who is steady, obedient, and fearless is the kind of man God uses to do a mighty work on the earth. Stepping forward is an act of war. It is a declaration that your life will no longer be governed by fear, passivity, or indecision. It is choosing faith over familiarity and obedience over comfort. God does not give strength to spectators; He gives strength to soldiers in motion. The moment you decide to act, grace meets you. Courage rises. Provision follows.

This is how God has always worked. He strengthens men after they step onto the battlefield, not before. God does not wait until a man feels ready before calling him to battle. He calls him while he is still trembling and then strengthens him after he steps forward. If God only sent men into battles they felt strong enough to fight, faith would never be required. Courage would be unnecessary. Dependence on God would be optional.

But the pattern of Scripture tells a different story: strength is released in motion, not in comfort. Many men believe God will empower them before the fight, before the temptation, before the confrontation, before the calling, before the risk. But that belief keeps them frozen at the edge of obedience, waiting for a feeling God never promised to give. Read the Word carefully. God rarely strengthens men in advance. He strengthens them in obedience. The warrior who waits to feel strong will wait forever but the warrior who moves in faith will discover strength he did not know he had.

Notice that the Red Sea did not part until the people moved forward. The walls of Jericho did not fall until the warriors marched around it. David wasn't empowered in the pasture to slay Goliath; he was strengthened when he stepped onto the battlefield. The giant did not fall until the stone was released. Gideon's courage didn't appear before the call; it grew as he obeyed. Peter didn't walk on water while sitting in the boat, but miracle-working strength met him after he stepped out. All these examples show us that God does not reward hesitation, but He always responds to faith. What this is all saying is that the world does not need more passive men. It needs men who will stand, decide, and move. Men who will lead their homes with integrity, serve their churches with courage, and confront darkness instead of avoiding it. You were born for this moment. The fire within you is not gone; it has simply been waiting for a decision. Draw the line in the sand. Step forward and do what you were born to do.

God has never failed to strengthen a man who dared to obey. The moment you step onto the battlefield - when your knees are shaking, your confidence thin, and your faith raw - that is where God meets you with power. Your destiny is calling out to you and it's time to step out of your comfort zone and into the unknown. Being a man and serving God is one big adventure and it begins right here. Pick up the call and put one foot in front of the other. It's time to man up and pursue God's calling with everything you've got. Solomon writes in Eccl. 5:3, "For a dream comes through much activity." Determine to never give up and keep going on the path you're currently on. You are more than a conqueror. You are strong in the Lord and the power of His might. Nothing can stop you now. The past is behind you, and the future is ever before you. Time is flying by. Don't let another day go by without doing something to pursue your call. Remember, you don't have to be great to start, but you have to start to be great.

Most men aren't stuck because they're weak. They're stuck because they're waiting to feel ready, waiting to feel worthy, waiting to feel confident, waiting until they "have it all together." That waiting room has claimed more dreams, callings, ministries, marriages, and destinies than failure ever has. The enemy doesn't need to destroy a man - he only needs to delay him. This is why all men need to understand that God has never called perfect men, only those willing to step forward when called upon to take their place in God's kingdom. From Genesis to Revelation, Scripture is packed with men who started flawed, unsure, and underqualified but God used them anyway. He didn't wait for them to feel great; He moved when they said yes to the call on their lives. "The LORD does not see as man sees; for man looks at the outward appearance, but the LORD looks at the heart" (1 Sam. 16:7) God isn't scanning your résumé - He's searching for availability. The starting line is where faith is proven.

Faith is not proven in comfort - it's proven in movement; in the actions you take. You don't build courage by thinking about courage, you don't build strength by reading about strength, and you don't build faith by waiting for faith. You build it by stepping forward while you're afraid. "Faith without works is dead" (James 2:17). Starting out and taking your place is an act of faith. Everybody is waiting for God to move first but in reality, it is God who is waiting for you to move. Why? Because confidence doesn't come before obedience - it comes from obedience. Every man wants confidence, but few men want the discomfort that produces it. David didn't gain confidence by visualizing Goliath's defeat; he gained it by picking up a sling and walking forward. "Then David ran toward the army to meet the Philistine" (1 Sam. 17:48). He ran before the victory. He moved before the outcome. Before this day is over, take one small step of obedience because God doesn't need your perfection, He needs your participation.

Men often underestimate the power of small beginnings. They want the platform without the preparation, the victory without the process, the testimony without the test. But God specializes in small starts. "Do not despise these small beginnings, for the LORD rejoices to see the work begin." (Zech. 4:10) Starting small does not mean thinking small. It means trusting God to grow what you place in His hands. Most men don't lack vision. They lack patience. They can see the finished product clearly - the restored marriage, the disciplined life, the spiritual authority, the legacy worth passing on. What frustrates them is not where they're going, but where they have to start. Beginnings feel beneath us. They feel unimpressive. Too slow. Too small to matter. That is why many men never move forward. They despise the beginning because it doesn't look like the end. They reject the small beginnings because they hunger only for the finished work. They reject the seed because it doesn't yet resemble the harvest.

The people of Israel felt the same way in the days of Zechariah. They had returned from exile and stood staring at the foundation of the rebuilt temple. It didn't compare to Solomon's glorious structure. Older men wept. Younger men felt discouraged. The work looked insignificant. But God did not rebuke the size of the project - He rebuked their attitude toward it. "Do not despise small beginnings." Why? Because God values beginnings more than appearances. The verse doesn't say the Lord rejoices when the work is finished. It says He rejoices when the work begins. This changes everything. God does not wait until you are strong to be pleased with you. He is pleased when you decide to take your place and start moving forward no matter how small the step may be. He rejoices when a man takes responsibility where he once avoided it, when he takes his place in God's kingdom. Heaven celebrates obedience, not the size of the step taken. What men often overlook, God openly celebrates.

Most men despise small beginnings because they measure progress incorrectly. They compare their chapter one to another man's chapter twenty. They confuse masculinity with speed and assume strength means instant results. But Scripture never defines manhood by how fast a man moves - it defines it by how faithfully he moves forward and endures when opposition comes. David wasn't crowned before he was faithful with sheep. Joseph didn't rule before he suffered in obscurity. Jesus didn't begin in public power; He began in private obedience. God always builds men from the inside out and from the ground up. Small beginnings are not a setback, but they are proof that God isn't finished with you yet, that there is still a call on your life. If you are still beginning, you are not late. If you are still starting over, you are not disqualified. A small beginning means God is not finished with you, that your story is still being written and the foundation of your calling is being laid correctly.

The enemy wants you to despise your small beginning, so you'll abandon the process. God wants you to honor your humble beginning, so you'll stay in it. Strong men are not those who never stumble but those who refuse to quit building. Later in Zech. 4:6 declares, "Not by might nor by power, but by My Spirit says the Lord." Small beginnings expose pride and force dependence on God. Small beginnings are not accidents. They are assignments. God often starts a man in places that feel beneath his calling, below his potential, and far from the vision burning in his heart. Why? Because small beginnings strip men of self-reliance. They remove the illusion that strength, talent, or experience is enough. When a man has little, he cannot hide behind ability. When resources are scarce, pride has nowhere to stand. When the task is bigger than one's own abilities, self-confidence collapses. Pride is often revealed where things begin small. Pride says, "I've got this." Small beginnings reply, "No, you don't."

Pride reveals how deeply a man trusts himself and how little he trusts God. It uncovers impatience, entitlement, and the secret belief that success should come quickly. In small beginnings motives are purified. Titles mean nothing. Applause is absent. The only thing left is obedience. And that is exactly where God does His deepest work. Small beginnings force dependence on God. When a man cannot rely on his own strength, he learns to rely on God's voice. When progress is slow, prayer becomes necessary, not optional. When the path is unclear, faith must replace control. God is not trying to embarrass a man in small beginnings - He is trying to train him. Self-reliance builds pride whereas dependence on God builds power. A man who skips small beginnings may look strong, but he will break under pressure. A man who endures them emerges grounded, teachable, and anchored in God. He knows the work was not achieved by his might, his wisdom, or his will but by the hand of God.

Small beginnings humble a man so God can trust him with more work and more responsibility. Do not despise where you are started and do not rush what God is using to reshape you. The place that feels limiting is often the place God is removing you from yourself so He can fully become your source. Remember, small beginnings are not a delay, they are divine preparation. Men who skip small beginnings often collapse under responsibility. But men who embrace them are forged for endurance. These are the men who change the world they live in, men who make a positive difference in the lives of others wherever they may go. A small beginning doesn't announce itself. It doesn't impress crowds. It rarely feels heroic. It may come as fifteen minutes of prayer instead of none, one chapter of scripture instead of excuses, one honest conversation with God, one act of restraint, one step of obedience when no one is watching. Consistency transforms what looks insignificant today into strength tomorrow.

Every great structure begins underground. Long before the walls rise and the skyline takes notice, there is a season no one applauds: a season of digging, a season of small beginnings. Foundations are formed in hidden places. The work is slow, messy, and often misunderstood. Dirt is moved. Rock is tested. Weak soil is removed. Nothing about it looks impressive, yet everything depends on it. God does His deepest work beneath the surface where motives are purified, character is strengthened, and roots are driven deep. He uses silence to teach trust. delay to build endurance, pressure to form strength. What feels like being buried is often the beginning of what is being built. A shallow foundation can only support a small structure. But when God plans something great, He digs deep. He allows small beginnings where progress seems invisible, where growth feels slow, and where faith must operate without applause. These seasons are not punishment; they are preparation.

Storms don't destroy buildings with strong foundations. Winds may howl and rains may fall, but what is anchored to bedrock stands firm. In the same way, trials reveal what depth has already been built within you. What God establishes in secret sustains you in public. If you find yourself in a small beginning where you're waiting, growing quietly, being shaped where no one sees - take heart. You are not being overlooked. You are being fortified. Every great structure begins underground and every life God intends to use powerfully is first built deeply. Rejoice knowing that God finishes what He starts. Phil. 1:6 says, "Being confident of this, that He who began a good work in you will carry it on to completion until the day of Christ Jesus." God does not abandon small beginnings. What He begins, He completes - not always quickly, but always faithfully. You are not called to rush the work. You are called to remain faithful to it. Progress that lasts is built slowly, deliberately, and under God's direction.

If God rejoices to see the work begin, then you should too. Stop despising where God has you and stop disqualifying yourself because progress feels slow. Honor the beginning, trust the process, and respect the Builder. The man who honors the foundation his life and calling are built upon will stand firm when the storm comes. Do not quit at the starting line and do not abandon the work because it looks small. God is still building, and He is not finished with you. Greatness isn't a gift - it's a journey that begins with obedience. Many want the crown, but few want the commands that come before it. We admire the finish line without honoring the footsteps that lead there. But in the Kingdom of God, greatness does not begin with recognition; it begins with submission. It begins with small beginnings. The journey will stretch you. It will test your patience. It will require humility and perseverance. But obedience always leads toward maturity, toward authority, and toward a life that truly matters.

| 13 |

"A BETTER MAN"

Real men are on a journey to become a better man. One of the greatest lies men believe is that manhood is a destination - something you reach, achieve, or finally arrive at. Culture promotes the idea that once you have enough strength, status, or success, you have "made it." Scripture teaches something far different. Real men are not defined by arrival; they are defined by movement. A real man on fire for God understands that growth never stops. He knows that the moment he believes he has arrived is the moment he begins to drift. Pride freezes progress, but humility keeps a man moving forward. God is not forming statues; He is shaping lives. The apostle Paul, one of the strongest spiritual leaders in history, declared plainly that he had not yet arrived, but he was pressing forward. That mindset is the mark of a real man. Not complacent. Not stagnant. But pursuing. A real man knows that manhood is a process proven over time, not in a moment. It is a journey, not a performance. It is forged, not flaunted.

A real man is not concerned with how he looks, how he's perceived, and how strong he seems. He is concerned with who he is becoming. He understands that true strength is internal before it is external. The journey to becoming a better man requires honesty. You cannot grow beyond what you are willing to admit. God works with truth, not pretending. The moment a man removes the mask and admits his need for growth, transformation begins. This process includes learning to listen instead of reacting all the time, choosing discipline over impulse and taking responsibility instead of making excuses. These are not signs of weakness. They are marks of maturity. Every man wants growth, but few want the discomfort that comes with it. Growth stretches a man. It challenges habits. It exposes flaws. It confronts attitudes that once felt justified. But God does His deepest work in uncomfortable places. Just as muscles grow through resistance, character grows through pressure.

Trials are not interruptions to the journey; they are tools in the journey. A real man does not ask, "Why is this happening to me?" He asks, "What is God shaping in me through this?" Correction, discipline, and hardship are not signs of abandonment. They are evidence that God is invested in the man you are becoming. Some men grow older, but they do not grow better. They allow pain, disappointment, or failure to harden them. A real man refuses that path. Bitterness shrinks a man while growth expands him and makes him better than he was before. A real man learns from failure instead of living in it. He repents quickly, forgives freely, and moves forward humbly. He understands that carrying resentment weighs him down on a journey that requires endurance. Becoming a better man means allowing God to refine your heart - not just sharpen your edge. Strength without love becomes cruelty. Confidence without humility becomes arrogance. Discipline without grace becomes legalism.

God is not just making strong men - He is making whole men, better men who can take others from where they are to where God wants them to be. But before a man can lead others, he must learn to lead himself. The journey to becoming a better man begins internally. Real men take responsibility for their thoughts, words, actions, and reactions. They don't blame circumstances or people for the condition of their character. Self-leadership includes guarding your mind, controlling your speech, managing your time, and honoring your commitments. A man who cannot govern himself will struggle to guide anyone else. Self-rule is the first battlefield. If a man is ruled by impulse, pride, anger, or fear, those same forces will spill over into every relationship and responsibility he touches. A man who lacks inner discipline may speak loudly, but his life whispers confusion. But a man who submits himself to God's leadership becomes steady, trustworthy, and strong. This is the man others can trust and follow.

A real man understands that greatness is not measured by recognition, but by obedience. Many men chase affirmation while neglecting formation. But God shapes leaders in hidden places long before He ever places them in public roles. The journey is often quiet, often unseen, and often misunderstood but every faithful step matters. A real man stays the course even when no one is clapping. He knows that obedience today produces strength tomorrow. Becoming a better man is a life-long calling. There is no finish line for becoming a better man on this side of eternity. As long as a man has breath, he has purpose. As long as he walks with God, he has room to grow. The goal is not perfection - it is progress. Real men stay teach-able, they stay humble, and they stay hungry for truth. They understand that becoming a better man is not a season they're going through, but it is a calling they live out each and every day of their lives. They know that real men are not perfect men; they are progressing men.

A better man is a man who wakes up each day committed to growth, a man who refuses stagnation, a man who walks the journey with courage, discipline, and faith. Every meaningful journey begins with a destination. No man sets out on a trip hoping to "just see where he ends up." He chooses a direc-tion, studies the path, prepares for the cost, and commits to the destination. Yet when it comes to life - especially man-hood - many men are moving without any clear sense of where they're going. They are busy, but not purposeful. Strong, but not directed. Capable, but not fulfilled. They're drifting along not knowing if they're coming or going. Drifting is very subtle. It doesn't announce itself. It happens slowly, quietly, over time. Drifting is what occurs when a man lives reactively in-stead of intentionally. He responds to circumstances rather than shaping them. He wakes up, goes to work, pays bills, scrolls his phone, manages problems, and repeats the cycle. Life happens to him instead of being built by him.

No man plans to drift but many men do because they never choose the direction they want their life to take. Drifting produces frustration, passivity, and resentment. A drifting man may look fine on the outside, but inside he feels disconnected like something essential is missing. That "something" is purpose anchored to identity. Drifting is not neutral. If a man is not intentionally moving forward, he is slowly drifting backward. Modern culture has stripped manhood of clear meaning. Responsibility has been replaced with comfort. Courage has been replaced with convenience. Leadership has been replaced with self-interest. Men are told not to be too strong, don't be too decisive, don't carry too much responsibility, and don't expect too much of yourself. The result is confusion. When manhood is undefined, men become directionless. Men do not suffer most from lack of ability. They suffer from lack of identity clarity. Without identity, there is no compass. Without a compass, movement becomes wandering.

Identity always comes before direction. You will never consistently live beyond who you believe you are. A man's actions, decisions, habits, and boundaries all emerge from his internal self-definition. If a man believes he is a victim; he'll avoid responsibility. If he believes he is a consumer, he'll live for pleasure. If he believes he is a bystander, he'll stay passive. If he believes he is a survivor, He'll always settle for less. But when a man understands his true identity, his direction changes immediately. Identity answers life's most important questions: Why am I here? What am I responsible for? What kind of man am I becoming? What will my life produce? A man who knows who he is doesn't need constant motivation from others; he moves forward with internal conviction. He's a man who doesn't need to be constantly pushed. His drive doesn't come from applause, pressure, or pep talks. It rises from conviction that is deep, settled, and unshakable. When identity is clear, movement is automatic.

Men do not need to return to outdated stereotypes, nor do they need to abandon strength altogether. They need to rise into redeemed, purpose-driven manhood. There is a cry echoing through our homes, our churches, and our culture. It is not the loud cry of rebellion, nor the arrogant shout of pride. It is the quieter, deeper cry of men who were created for more but have settled for less. Men who were designed to carry responsibility, to stand in strength, to lead with love, and to walk in righteousness yet find themselves passive, distracted, wounded, or unsure of who they truly are. This is not a generation lacking masculinity. It is a generation lacking redeemed masculinity. Manhood is not a cultural invention - it is a divine calling. God did not create men to drift through life without direction. He formed men with intentionality, breathed purpose into them, and entrusted them with responsibility. From the beginning, man was called to work, to guard, to lead, and to walk with God.

Strength was never meant to be domination, and leadership was never meant to be selfish control. Biblical manhood was designed to be strong enough to protect and humble enough to serve. But when man steps away from God, he does not lose strength - he loses direction. And strength without direction becomes destructive. That is why the world is filled with men who are powerful but empty, driven but restless, successful but broken. When manhood is not redeemed, it often expresses itself in extremes. Some men harden their hearts and dominate. Others retreat into passivity and silence. Some numb themselves with pleasure, addiction, or endless distraction. Others chase success, hoping achievement will give them the identity they never settled in God. Unredeemed manhood wounds families. It leaves women carrying burdens they were never meant to carry alone. It leaves children longing for guidance, affirmation, and presence. It leaves churches with men who attend but do not engage.

The answer is not shaming men. The answer is calling them higher, to man up and become better men. Redemption does not erase masculinity - it restores it. When a man encounters God, he does not become weaker; he becomes whole. Redemption heals the wounds that caused fear, pride, anger, and withdrawal. It restores a man's identity so he no longer has to prove himself, perform for approval, or hide behind false strength. A redeemed man knows who he is in Christ. He does not need to dominate those around him because he is secure in his identity as a man of God. He does not need to run away from his responsibilities because he has purpose. He understands that true strength is the ability to stand when it is easier to run, to remain faithful when compromise is convenient, and to lead with integrity when no one is watching. Men are wired for purpose. A man who knows why he's here is anchored to the bedrock of masculinity. He becomes a better man, the man he was created to be.

When a man lacks purpose, he becomes restless but when he understands his divine purpose, the reason he exists, his life begins to align with the will of God. Purpose-driven manhood is not about personal ambition - it is about divine assignment. It is the understanding that your life is not your own, that your strength is meant to serve something greater than yourself. A purpose-driven man asks, "What has God entrusted to me? How can my life honor God and bless others?" Purpose steadies a man in chaos. It gives him resolve in hardship and clarity in confusion. It turns survival into stewardship. No man rises into redeemed manhood accidentally. It requires intentional surrender and courageous responsibility. Rising means a man stops blaming his past and starts stewarding his future. It means he takes ownership of his thoughts, his words, his actions, and his influence. He does not excuse his weaknesses; he submits them to God for transformation.

Responsibility is not a burden to avoid; it is a mantle to embrace. A burden is something laid on a man against his will. A mantle is something placed upon him by God - a calling that signifies trust, authority, and purpose. God entrusts weight only to those He intends to strengthen and use mightily. Too many men run from responsibility because they've been told it will crush them. But scripture shows that responsibility is what forms a man. Responsibility sharpens vision and awakens courage. From the beginning, God entrusted man with responsibility. Adam was placed in the garden to tend it and keep it. Responsibility was not a curse of the fall; it was a gift of design. When God called men throughout scripture, He did not remove weight from their shoulders - He added purpose to their strength. David was given a kingdom to shepherd. Nehemiah was given a broken wall to rebuild. Joseph was given authority to preserve a nation. None of them were crushed by responsibility; they were revealed by it.

The enemy tells men that responsibility will rob them of freedom. But the truth is that irresponsibility enslaves, while responsibility establishes dominion. A man who avoids responsibility remains small, restless, and unstable. A man who embraces it grows rooted, steady, and strong. Responsibility is the mantle that separates men from boys. It is not something to drop when it feels heavy; it is something to grow into. God never places a mantle without also providing the grace to carry it. Real men don't ask God to remove the weight they've been commanded to carry, they ask. "Lord, make me strong enough to carry what You've given me." When a man embraces responsibility, he reflects the heart of Christ who carried the greatest weight of all, not because it was easy, but because love required it. Responsibility doesn't exist to restrain you - it exists to reveal you. It's the weight that forges strength, the assignment that gives your life direction. Responsibility is not your prison. It is your calling.

What feels heavy is often holy; what demands discipline is usually preparing you for influence. Responsibility isn't a chain meant to hold you back - it's a summons for you to step up, stand firm, and become the man you were created to be. When you embrace responsibility, you don't lose your freedom, you discover your purpose. You discover that all men were made by God to be steadfast and stand strong. To man up and become a better man means you'll stand in truth when lies are popular, you'll stand in love when anger is rewarded, and you'll stand in faith when fear dominates the atmosphere. Redeemed men do not abandon their post. They stand for their families. They stand for righteousness. They stand for the vulnerable. They stand up strong for what is right even when it costs them comfort, convenience, or reputation. They are not perfect, but they are present. They are not flawless, but they are steadfast and faithful. They are not driven by ego but by their heavenly calling.

True manhood is not arrogance; it is responsibility embraced. True strength is not dominance; it is discipline. True leadership is not control; it is service guided by conviction. A real man will man up and accept responsibility instead of avoiding it. He chooses discipline over comfort, builds rather than consumes, protects what matters, and finishes what he starts. This identity does not shrink men; it anchors them and makes them strong. When a man knows that he was created to build, protect, lead, and leave a legacy, his life gains direction. Now is the time for men to rise up and become better men - not in arrogance, but in humility; not in domination, but in devotion; not in self-reliance, but in surrendered strength. The world does not need men who merely exist. It needs men who are redeemed, anchored, awake, and purpose driven. Rise up into the man you were created to be. Rise up above passivity, rise up into responsibility, and rise up into your calling. Rise up into purpose-driven manhood.

The world is waiting for all men to become better men. When they man up their families are strengthened, their communities are stabilized, faith becomes visible, and the next generation finds direction. Men who know who they are and why they're here do not quit when the road gets difficult. They adjust, endure, and advance forward because they know the destination is worth the cost. Every man must decide, "Will I drift or will I lead? Will I react or will I build? Will I remain undefined or step into who I was created to be?" Manhood is not about perfection. It is about direction. Direction begins when a man decides that wandering is no longer acceptable, when he commits to becoming intentional about his character, his responsibilities, and his legacy. It's when he draws a line in the sand and says with conviction, "Wandering ends here." Direction comes when drifting is no longer tolerated and when excuses give way to intention. Clarity doesn't come from movement alone; it comes from commitment.

A man finds direction when he chooses to shape his character on purpose, shoulder his responsibilities with resolve, and live with his legacy in mind. A man who knows where he's going may stumble but he will not be lost. Even the strongest men misstep, lose footing, or face moments of weakness. But direction changes everything. When a man knows his purpose - when his heart is fixed on where he's headed - every fall becomes a lesson, not a dead end. Progress is not proven by never falling, but by always getting back up and continuing forward. The journey of manhood does not begin with external change. It begins with an internal declaration that says, "I will no longer drift. I will no longer live undefined. I will become the man I was created to be." When a man finds his identity, his direction becomes clear. And when his direction becomes clear, his life begins to move with power, purpose, and re-solve. Know who you are, know where you're going, and walk forward with intention. The journey starts now.

| 14 |

"AUTHENTIC MANHOOD"

The future you want is connected to the man you choose to be today. Not the image you project, not the reputation you defend, not the version of yourself shaped by culture, wounds, or convenience. Your future is linked to authentic manhood - the kind that is forged in truth, humility, courage, and obedience to God. Every generation rises or falls on the strength of its men. Homes rise or fall. Churches rise or fall. Nations rise or fall. And the determining factor is not power, money, charisma, or talent - it is the character of its men. Authentic manhood is not loud, arrogant, or domineering. It does not posture or pretend. It does not hide behind excuses or shift blame. Authentic manhood is honest about weakness, fierce about responsibility, and anchored in God's design. When men abandon authenticity, the future pays the price. When men walk in God's design, the future is strengthened. If you want a better future for yourself, your family, your church, and the next generation, this is where the journey begins.

God never designed men to drift. He designed them to lead, steward, protect, and build. The problem men face today is we are living in a time of confusion about what it means to be a man. In the 1990's a Michael Jordan commercial encouraged people to "be like Mike." A young boy said, "I want to grow up to be a real man like Michael Jordan." Another boy said, "Not me. I want to grow up to be a real man - just like my mom." This is a sad commentary to the condition of manhood in the world today. Counterfeit manhood avoids responsibility or abuses it. It seeks control instead of calling. Confused men deny reality. They pretend everything is okay. They sweep things under the rug. From birth to late teens, most children are raised by women, many of whom are single mothers. At home, women are the dominate authority figure. Mothers tell the children to clean their room and what clothes to wear. It's the wife who usually pays the bills. Worst of all, there are more women in church today than men.

Where are all the men at? The problem is there is no clear picture of what a real man is really like. Some voices tell men to be passive, silent, and apologetic. Others tell men to be aggressive, selfish, and unaccountable. Both paths are counterfeit and both lead to destruction. Most men today are drifting and disappointed with life. As strong as men appear to be, most men are fragile, confused, and lonely. Men have no clear understanding of who they are and what they are supposed to do. The reality of life is that confused men settle for less. They settle into an empty rut because they don't know what else to live for. They don't have a higher calling in life other than themselves and that don't fill and satisfy the void they feel in their life. There is no lofty vision of manhood that is compelling to men. TV programs and commercials portray men as wimps, idiots, and bumbling morons. This creates a vacuum that is killing manhood as God intended it to be. There is no vision calling us up from boyhood.

Like a giant tsunami a masculine meltdown is sweeping across the land today and God is saying "No more!" He is commanding all men to man up and show the world what a man of God is really like. He is calling you to rise up and seize your manhood. For that to happen the boy in you must die! All over the world there are 40 yr. old, 50 yr. old, and 60 yr. old boys. There needs to be an immediate transition from boyhood to manhood. 1 Cor. 13:11, "When I was a child, I spoke as a child, I thought as a child; but when I became a man, I put away childish things." The Message Bible says, "When I was an infant at my mother's breast, I gurgled and cooed like any infant. When I grew up, I left those infant ways for good." Authentic manhood starts with knowing the truth about God, about yourself, and about your responsibility as a man. Real men do not fear the truth, they welcome it. Truth strips away pretense. It exposes motives. It confronts excuses. And while truth may wound the ego, it heals the soul.

Authentic manhood starts where honesty begins - with God. Ps. 139:23 says, "Search me, O God, and know my heart! Try me and know my thoughts." Real men invite examination. They don't fear truth because they trust the One who reveals it. A man who lives in denial of the truth cannot grow just like a man who lives in deception cannot lead. A man who refuses truth cannot secure a better future for himself and his loved ones. Authentic men live examined lives. They invite God to search their hearts. They submit to correction. They understand that repentance is not weakness, it is strength under control. The future belongs to men who are honest enough to face today as it really is. Correction is not rejection - it is an investment into your calling as a man of God. Men who resist truth remain boys in character but men who embrace truth mature into leaders. Jesus said, "You will know the truth, and the truth will set you free" (John 8:32). Freedom is not found in pretending - it is found in authenticity.

Authentic manhood draws strength from God, not ego. The world defines strength as dominance, toughness, and emotional distance. God defines strength differently. Biblical strength is not the absence of emotion - it is mastery over it. It is not the absence of fear - it is obedience in spite of it. It is not independence - it is dependence on God. The world praises outward power while God values inner mastery. Prov. 16:32 says, "Better is a man who rules his spirit than one who takes a city." The world applauds visible victories. Cities conquered. Enemies defeated. Titles earned. Crowds impressed. But Scripture pulls back the curtain and reveals a deeper, greater triumph - the victory within. God declares that a man who rules his own spirit is greater than a warrior who captures a city. Why? Because cities fall from the outside, but a man falls from the inside. Any man can lash out in anger. Any man can surrender to impulse, pride, fear, or lust. But it takes a strong, God-trained man to govern his spirit.

Uncontrolled emotions turn strong men into weak ones. Rage ruins families. Impulses destroy callings. Pride blinds leaders. Fear paralyzes destiny. The enemy doesn't need to defeat a man publicly if he can first conquer him privately. Prov. 16:32 says, "He who is slow to anger is better than the mighty." Strength in God's kingdom is not measured by how loudly a man roars, but by how firmly he stands when everything in him wants to react. A man who rules his spirit walks in authority. He is not driven by mood, manipulated by offense, or enslaved by appetite. He chooses wisdom over impulse, obedience over emotion, and discipline over comfort. The apostle Paul echoes this truth in 1 Cor. 9:27, "I discipline my body and bring it into subjection." Self-control is not weakness -it is mastery over fleshly impulses. It is the fruit of the Spirit at work within a surrendered life (Gal/5:22–23). When the Holy Spirit rules a man's heart, that man learns to rule himself.

History is filled with conquerors who ruled nations but could not rule themselves. Their empires collapsed because their inner life was in chaos. God is not impressed by outward dominance when inward discipline is absent. A man may win arguments and lose his marriage. He may gain influence and lose integrity. He may conquer others and yet be conquered by sin. But the man who rules his spirit builds strong homes, earns lasting trust, walks in peace, leads with clarity and courage, and finishes his race well. Jesus was the perfect example of a man with strength under control. He could calm storms, command angels, and silence demons yet He chose restraint when the situation called for it. He did not react in anger, panic in pressure, or retaliate in injustice. At the cross, true strength was on display when He allowed Himself to be beaten and ridiculed. He had power under control. 1 Peter 2:23 says, "When He was reviled, he did not revile in return." That is the strength God calls all men to pursue.

Ruling your spirit is not automatic - it is intentional. It requires prayer, humility, accountability, and submission to God's Word. It means pausing before reacting, listening before speaking, and obeying God even when emotions resist. This is the mark of real manhood. This the warrior God honors. This is the victory heaven celebrates. Better is the man who rules his spirit than one who takes a city because the greatest conquest is the soul surrendered to God. The greatest conquest a man will ever face is not across a battlefield, a boardroom, or a city wall. It is the conquest of the heart. When the soul is surrendered to God, chaos gives way to order. When the spirit is governed by the Holy Spirit, reactions become responses, passions find purpose, and strength is guided by wisdom. Cities can be rebuilt. Kingdoms can rise and fall. But a surrendered soul becomes a dwelling place for God Himself. This is the man who does not need to prove his strength; it is evident in his restraint, his obedience, and his peace.

In the end, the greatest victory is not what a man conquers for God, but what he allows God to conquer in him. For when God rules the soul, the man is finally free and that victory echoes into eternity. We admire outward triumphs - battles won, ministries built, mountains climbed, enemies defeated. Yet heaven measures victory by a different standard. God is not impressed by how much we accomplish in His name if our hearts remain unconquered by His rule. The true battlefield has always been the inner man. Scripture reminds us that "the kingdom of God is within you" (Luke 17:21). Before God advances His purposes through a man, He must first reign over the man. Pride must bow. Fear must yield. Self-will must surrender. Hidden sin must be exposed. This is not weakness - it is the bravest form of warfare a man will ever fight. Authentic strength is self-governed strength. It is the ability to restrain anger, resist temptation, and remain faithful under pressure.

Many want God's power without God's authority. They want victory without surrender, strength without submission, freedom without obedience. But the truth be told, a man is never more free than when God fully rules him. 2 Cor. 3:17 says, "Where the Spirit of the Lord is, there is freedom." When God conquers the heart, chains fall that no external victory could ever break. The need to prove oneself fades. The fear of man loses its grip. The tyranny of the flesh is dethroned. What once ruled the man now serves him, because God reigns. The man who allows God to conquer him becomes dangerous to darkness and secure in identity. He no longer fights to be seen, validated, or remembered. He fights from a place of rest, obedience, and eternal purpose. As time passes trophies rust and applause fades but inner transformation endures. The greatest victory is not written in headlines or history books. It is written in heaven, where a surrendered life stands as eternal proof that God reigns supreme.

A man whose heart is controlled by the Holy Spirit rises up and embraces the responsibility that falls on every man. A real man looks for assignments to do for he understands that responsibility is not a burden to resent but it is a calling to fulfill. A masculine man takes responsibility for his walk with God, his words and actions, his family and relationships, and his influence and example. He does not blame his past, his parents, his circumstances, or society. He understands that while he may not control what happened to him, he does control what kind of man he becomes. Every time a man steps up and accepts responsibility, he strengthens the bridge to a better future. Every time he avoids it, he weakens that bridge. Authentic men do not run from responsibility; they rise to it. 1 Cor. 4:2 says, "It is required of stewards that they be found faithful." A man may not control every circumstance, but he controls his response. He knows that responsibility embraced today prevents regret tomorrow.

From the beginning, God built man with responsibility in mind. Gen. 2:15 says, "The Lord God took the man and put him in the garden of Eden to work it and keep it." Before Adam had a wife, before he had children, before there was sin in the world, there was responsibility. God entrusted Adam with care, protection, and stewardship. Responsibility was not a result of the fall, rather it was part of God's original design. A man is not weakened by responsibility; he is formed by it. Just as muscles grow by resisting weight, a man of God is strengthened by carrying what God entrusts to him. Responsibility is not what crushes a man - it is what constructs him. 1 Cor. 16:13 says, "Be watchful, stand firm in the faith, act like men, be strong." Paul does not tell men to escape responsibility; he tells them to stand under the weight of it. Why? Because responsibility is God's tool that brings about maturity and authentic manhood. A man of God accepts responsibility and embraces it as an assignment from on high.

Spiritual immaturity is often revealed by how quickly a man resents the weight of responsibility. At the same time, maturity is revealed by how willingly he carries it. A truth to be grasped onto is the weight you carry shapes the man you become. God does not develop men in comfort zones. He develops them under the weight they carry. David did not become king by avoiding responsibility. He embraced it when no one was watching, when he was guarding sheep, facing lions, and protecting what belonged to his father. That weight prepared him for Goliath. The responsibilities you accept today are training you for battles you haven't faced yet. Every burden carried faithfully adds strength to your spiritual character. Jesus Himself modeled this truth. He said in Mark 10:45, "For even the Son of Man did not come to be served, but to serve, and to give His life as a ransom for many." The strongest man who ever lived carried the heaviest responsibility imaginable - the salvation of the world.

Avoiding responsibility weakens a man. He may feel lighter, but he becomes fragile. A man who refuses responsibility becomes easily offended, easily discouraged, easily tempted, and easily broken. Why? Because responsibility anchors a man. It gives him purpose, direction, and identity. When a man knows what he is accountable for - his faith, his family, his integrity, his calling - he stands strong when the storms of life come. God entrusts more to men who prove faithful with what they already carry. Matt. 25:21 says, "Well done, good and faithful servant, you were faithful over a few things, I will make you ruler over many things." Responsibility may feel heavy, but it stabilizes the soul. It sharpens discernment. It builds resilience. It teaches a man to depend on God rather than drift through life untethered. So do not fear responsibility. Fear the weakness that comes from refusing it. Carry what God has given you. Stand where He has placed you. Bear the weight and become strong.

Authentic manhood accepts the fact that integrity is the backbone of tomorrow. Integrity is not loud. It doesn't announce itself or demand applause. Yet it carries the weight of the future on its shoulders. The life in front of you is being quietly framed by the integrity - or the lack of it - of men today. Integrity is the backbone of tomorrow because it holds everything upright when pressure increases. Without a backbone, a body collapses. Without integrity, a life bends, a family wobbles, and a nation loses its posture. Talent may open doors, charisma may win crowds, and strength may conquer obstacles but only integrity sustains what time and trials test. A man without integrity may move faster, but he builds on sand. He may gain in the short term, but he mortgages the future. Integrity, on the other hand, is patient. It chooses obedience when compromise would be easier. It does what is right when no one is watching. Authentic manhood refuses to live divided. The private man and the public man are the same man.

Prov. 11:3 says, "The integrity of the upright guides them, but the perversity of the unfaithful will destroy them." Integrity is guidance for the unseen road ahead. It is a compass that keeps a man aligned when the culture pulls him sideways. Tomorrow's marriages will stand or fall on the integrity practiced today. Tomorrow's children will either trust or doubt based on the truth they see lived out now. Tomorrow's legacy is not shaped by intentions, but by consistent character. Integrity is the silent promise that a man's word can be trusted, and his life will match his confession. Integrity also strengthens the inner man. It creates spiritual stability that doesn't panic in storms or crumble under temptation. When integrity is present, peace follows, because there is no double life to maintain and no mask to protect. God builds futures on men who are whole, not divided. Integrity weaves belief and behavior into one unbreakable strand. When integrity stands firm today, tomorrow will stand tall.

While integrity is the backbone of tomorrow, it's courage that transforms the future. Authentic manhood requires courage - not the reckless courage of impulse, but the steady courage of conviction. Men need courage to stand when it would be easier to sit, speak when silence feels safer, obey when compromise looks profitable, and change when pride says stay the same. Courage is contagious. One man's courage strengthens others. One man's stand can alter the direction of a family, a church, or a generation. The future is never changed by men who drift - it is changed by men who decide to live a courageous life. A better future is not accidental. It is intentional. And authenticity is the foundation it rests on. Man up and bear the responsibility of being a man of God. You the link between what was and what will be, between confusion and clarity. God is still looking for men who understand that authentic manhood is not just about who they are today, but about the future they are shaping.

| 15 |

"THE BUCK STOPS HERE"

From the very beginning, God established a divine order for leadership and responsibility. When chaos entered the world through sin, God did not first call out to Eve - He called out to Adam saying, "Adam, where are you?" (Gen. 3:9). That question echoes through every generation of men. God was not asking for Adam's location; He was calling him to give an account for what happened. This reveals the powerful truth that the solution to life's problems begins with the man. God designed men to take responsibility, to initiate action, and to stand in the gap when things go wrong. Leadership is not domination, and responsibility is not tyranny - it is ownership. A man who takes charge does not blame others, make excuses, or retreat when pressure rises. He steps forward knowing that in the Kingdom of God, maturity and authentic manhood is marked by a simple but powerful declaration, "The buck stops here." In other words, every man must answer for his own obedience before God.

This statement is not about pride or control. It is not about claiming authority over everything or pretending to have all the answers. It is about accountability. It is the spiritual declaration that a man understands his role, accepts his assignment, and refuses to hide behind excuses. From the very beginning, responsibility was woven into man's design. God placed Adam in the garden not merely to enjoy it, but to tend it and keep it. Before sin ever entered the world, man was given responsibility. Leadership was not a consequence of the fall; it was part of God's original intent. When Adam disobeyed God, something revealing happened. Instead of owning his failure, Adam blamed Eve. Eve, in turn, blamed the serpent. This pattern of deflection did not lessen their guilt. God did not accept their excuses. He addressed each one personally. The lesson was unmistakable: no man escapes responsibility by shifting blame. God deals with individuals based on what they were entrusted with, not on who influenced them.

Yes, influence may explain behavior, but it never removes accountability. Blaming others for one's failures is one of the greatest enemies of spiritual growth. A man who blames never matures because he never learns. As long as responsibility is transferred elsewhere, transformation is delayed. Blame weakens men in subtle ways. It creates a false sense of innocence while quietly stripping away authority. A man who refuses responsibility cannot be trusted with greater responsibility. Heaven does not promote excuse-makers. Scripture repeatedly shows that when leaders avoided responsibility, chaos followed. When responsibility was embraced, restoration began. God's correction often started with a simple question, "Where are you?" This wasn't asked because God lacked information, but because He wanted Adam to take ownership of what he did. Many men have the desire for authority without the responsibility that goes with it. They want influence without accountability and power without burden.

On the other hand, a man who accepts responsibility becomes stable. His words carry weight because they are backed by action. His leadership brings order because he does not run when pressure comes. Responsibility is the price of authority, and authority is the reward of faithfulness. This is why God tested men before trusting them. David was responsible for sheep before he was trusted with a kingdom. Moses was responsible for a flock before he was entrusted with a nation. Responsibility precedes promotion. No one modeled responsibility more clearly than Jesus Christ. Though sinless, He accepted responsibility for sinners. He did not blame humanity for its brokenness - He bore the cost of it. He did not distance Himself from the problem - He became the solution. Jesus did not avoid the cross; He embraced it. He did not shift the burden; He carried it. In doing so, He redefined strength. True strength is not avoiding responsibility - it is embracing it with obedience.

Every man who follows Christ is called to walk in this same spirit. Accepting responsibility is not about control; it is about obedience. It is not about ego; it is about submission to God's will Accepting responsibility changes how a man lives daily. It affects his choices, his reactions, and his priorities. A responsible man does not ask, "Who can I blame?" like Adam did. Instead, he asks, "What does God require of me?' A man who accepts responsibility becomes a point of stability in unstable environments. His home feels the difference. His workplace sees the difference. His church benefits from the difference. God does not hold men responsible for what they were never given but He absolutely holds them responsible for what they were. Every man is accountable for his obedience, his attitude, and his response to truth. Responsibility begins internally, in the heart of a man. It starts with thoughts, decisions, and discipline. External leadership collapses without internal accountability.

A man cannot lead others well if he refuses to lead himself. This is why repentance is powerful. Repentance is responsibility in action. It is the refusal to justify sin and the willingness to change direction. While sorrow may awaken the conscience, repentance is what proves the heart has changed. To repent is to stop explaining sin and start confronting it. It is the refusal to justify what God has already condemned and the courage to turn away from what once felt familiar. Repentance is ownership. It does not blame circumstances, childhood wounds, pressure, temptation, or other people. It does not soften sin with excuses or rename disobedience as weakness. Repentance stands in the light and says, "This is on me. By God's grace, the buck stops here." That moment is not defeat; it is the beginning of strength, real strength, the strength that turns a boy into a man. To repent literally means to change direction. It is not merely turning away from sin but turning toward God.

Repentance is a reorientation of the will. The feet that once walked toward darkness now walk toward truth. The mind that once justified compromise now submits to obedience. The heart that once resisted correction now welcomes it. True repentance always produces action. It restores what was broken, corrects what was wrong, and abandons what dishonors God. It does not negotiate with sin or attempt to manage it. Instead, it removes it. Where repentance is genuine, patterns change, priorities shift, and fruit appears. Repentance is proof of spiritual maturity and authentic manhood. Boys make excuses; men take responsibility. Children hide; sons return home. Repentance is not weakness - it is moral courage. It is the strength to say no to the flesh and yes to God, even when it costs pride, comfort, or reputation. God always responds to it. Heaven moves when a man takes responsibility for his sin and chooses righteousness instead. Grace does not excuse rebellion; it empowers transformation.

Repentance is the doorway through which that grace flows. In the end, repentance is not about condemnation - it is about restoration. It is God's invitation to leave what destroys and step into what gives life. Repentance is responsibility in action, change in motion, a heart aligned again with heaven. Every man must eventually draw a line in the sand. It is the moment he decides once and for all that he will no longer delay obedience, shift blame, or wait for someone else to lead. This moment defines authentic manhood. When a man declares, "The buck stops here," he is declaring war on passivity. He is rejecting being a victim of life by choosing responsibility over resignation. He is embracing his God-given role with humility and courage. This declaration does not make life easier, but it does makes it more meaningful. Yes, responsibility is heavy, but it also frees the soul. When a man accepts responsibility, he gains clarity. When he gains clarity, he gains peace. When he gains peace, he gains strength.

God entrusts more to men who can carry weight without complaint. Heaven looks for shoulders strong enough to bear responsibility and hearts humble enough to obey. From the beginning, God designed men to own the moment, not escape it. Responsibility is not a burden - it is a calling. It is the mark of maturity, strength, and godly leadership. The mark of a godly man is not perfection, but ownership. When a man stops pointing fingers and starts saying, "This is on me," something powerful happens inside him. In a world full of excuses, blame, and avoidance, the man who accepts responsibility stands out. He becomes dependable. He becomes influential. He becomes trustworthy. And when life presses him, when questions come, and when decisions must be made, he does not look around for someone else to step forward. He steps forward himself and declares before God and others, "The buck stops here." People know where he stands. His word carries weight because his life backs it up.

A man who is dependable does not disappear when pressure rises or when things go wrong. He shows up. He stays engaged. Like Nehemiah rebuilding the wall or Joseph stewarding Egypt, God entrusts more to the man who proves faithful with what is already in his hands. When others retreat, he advances. When pressure increases, he remains steady. When things fall apart, he holds his ground. In the world today dependability is a rare thing and therefore has become a priceless virtue. Families depend on it. Churches rely on it. Communities are stabilized by it. A dependable man does not make excuses when things go wrong. He asks, "What can I do? What needs to change? How can I lead through this?" We live in an age of broken promises. Commitments are made lightly and abandoned quickly. Words are spoken without weight, and responsibility is often shifted instead of shouldered. Because of this, the man who can be counted on immediately stands apart. God entrusts weight to men who can carry it.

Dependability builds trust. Trust is not created by talent, charisma, or good intentions - it is forged through consistency. When people know you will show up, follow through, and stand firm even when it costs you, your words gain authority. Your presence carries weight. Your influence grows naturally. Influence is not demanded - it is earned. Others begin to follow you not because of position, volume, or force, but because you continually keep your word. Responsibility gives a man moral authority. When he leads his home, his work, and his walk with God with ownership and humility, people listen. Leadership flows naturally from responsibility. Men who accept responsibility gain the respect of others because their lives demonstrate consistency. They do not need to announce leadership; it is evident in how they live. Influence grows when words align with actions, when promises are kept, and when responsibility is taken. People follow men they can trust. Consistency creates that trust.

Dependability reflects the character of God Himself. God is faithful even when people are not. He keeps covenant. He does not change with moods, seasons, or circumstances. When a man walks in dependability, he mirrors the nature of the God he serves. He becomes a living testimony of divine faithfulness in a shaky world. A dependable person becomes a pillar in the community. He becomes someone others lean on when pressure comes. Dependability is not about perfection; it is about integrity. It means doing what you said you would do, even when it's inconvenient. It means standing your post when others walk away. It means being steady when everything else is uncertain. In times of confusion and compromise, the dependable believer shines like a lighthouse. He may not be the loudest voice in the room, but he is often the most trusted. And in the kingdom of God, faithfulness opens doors that talent never could. Choose to be dependable. In a world that wavers, let your life be firm.

A responsible man becomes trustworthy. Trust is heaven's currency. Scripture teaches that faithfulness in small things precedes faithfulness in greater ones. God looks for men He can trust - men who will carry truth, guard integrity, and stand firm when compromise is easier. He watches how men handle what is already in their hands, things like their marriages, their children, their work, their integrity, their obedience. Responsibility proves character. It reveals a man who can be counted on when it matters most. Adam fell not because he lacked ability, but because he avoided responsibility. Christ redeemed us by fully embracing it. Where Adam shifted blame, Jesus carried the cross. Where Adam hid, Jesus stepped forward. That is the pattern of true manhood. A man who is responsible says, "I will take the lead. I will carry the weight. I will answer the call." The man who accepts responsibility becomes rare and therefore powerful. He becomes trustworthy, the kind of man God is pleased to use.

When a man says, "The buck stops here," he is not claiming perfection - he is claiming ownership. He is saying, "I may not control everything, but I am responsible for what I do control. I will stand before God accountable for my choices." Scripture repeatedly affirms this truth. Leaders were judged not for what others did, but for what they allowed. Fathers were held accountable for what they modeled. Kings were corrected for what they tolerated. Responsibility is never optional in God's economy. Jesus Himself demonstrated ultimate responsibility. Though sinless, He took responsibility for sinners. He did not pass the burden - He carried it. He did not deflect the cost - He paid it. He went to the cross saying, "The buck stops here." And because of His example, every believer is called to live with the same weight of ownership. Accepting responsibility changes everything. It turns boys into men. It turns excuses into repentance. It turns chaos into order. It turns weakness into authority.

A man who accepts responsibility becomes a stabilizing force. His home feels safer. His words carry weight. His prayers gain power. Heaven trusts him because he does not run when things get hard. Taking charge does not mean controlling others - it means controlling yourself. It means refusing to blame, refusing to hide, and refusing to disengage. A responsible man leads with humility, decides with courage, and serves with strength. God is not asking men to be flawless - He is asking them to be faithful. He is not looking for perfection, but participation. The world does not need louder opinions; it needs men who will stand up and take responsibility. When a man takes charge of his walk with God, his home stabilizes. When a man takes charge of his calling, others find direction. When a man takes charge of responsibility, God releases power. The solution to life's problems does not begin with policies, systems, or circumstances. It begins with a man who will stand and say, "I am responsible."

When men man up, everything changes. God designed men to take charge of life's situations. The solution to life's problems begins with the man. Homes, churches, and nations are only as strong as the men in their midst. True manhood doesn't come with age but with the acceptance of responsibility. A childish man is one who refuses to take responsibility for his life and actions. When men abandon their God-given role, confusion fills the vacuum. But when men rise to take responsibility, order follows. Many of life's crises - broken homes, lost direction, spiritual drift - can be traced back to abdicated leadership. When a man refuses to lead, someone else will step in, often without the authority or covering God intended. God's design was never for men to be passive observers; He created them to be initiators, protectors, and problem-solvers. A man who accepts this calling looks life square in the face and declares before God and others, "The buck stops here."

God's design for men was never passive. He did not create men to be spectators of life, standing on the sidelines while families crumble, truth erodes, and responsibility is avoided. From the beginning, God formed men to step forward, not step back - to initiate, protect, and solve problems, not wait for someone else to act. Throughout Scripture, God consistently calls men to move first. Noah built the ark while others mocked. Abraham left familiarity and stepped into the unknown. Moses confronted Pharaoh. David ran toward the giant. Nehemiah rebuilt what had been broken. Jesus Himself did not wait for darkness to retreat - He advanced the Kingdom of God with authority, truth, and sacrificial strength. Biblical masculinity is not about domination; it is about ownership. Ownership of responsibility. Ownership of decisions. Ownership of consequences. Real men don't ask, "Who will fix this?" They ask, " What has God entrusted to me? What has God commanded me to do?"

All men are called to be problem-solvers. They're designed to protect and stand watch over their homes, their marriages, their children, and their faith. When walls are broken, men rebuild. When chaos rises, men bring order. When fear spreads, men stand firm. God wired men with the ability to confront reality, make hard decisions, and carry weight - not to escape pressure, but to bear it with strength and faith. Passivity shrinks men. Responsibility sharpens them. The world does not need more disengaged men waiting for direction - it needs men who listen to God and act. Men who pray boldly, lead courageously, love sacrificially, and stand unwaveringly. Men who refuse to be spectators in a battle God has already called them to fight. God's design has never changed. Men were created to rise, to lead, to protect, and to build. Not because they are superior but because that is what their assignment is. The call still stands. Man up and be the man God designed you to be. The buck stops here.

| 16 |

"ANCHORED MEN"

Good men are needed in the world like never before. The world is not suffering from a lack of information, innovation, or opinion - it is suffering from a lack of good men. Needed are men who will stand when it's easier to sit, men who will speak truth when silence feels safer, and men who will lead with humility, courage, and conviction when culture rewards passivity and compromise. From the beginning, God's design was clear: men were created to guard, cultivate, and guide. Adam was placed in the garden to protect what God entrusted to him. That calling has never been revoked. What has changed is the resistance against it. Today, confusion replaces clarity. Weakness is applauded while strength is mocked. Responsibility is avoided, and accountability is resented. Into this moment, God is still calling for good men to rise up and make this world a better place. Good men are anchors in unstable times. They protect the vulnerable. They love their families sacrificially and take on responsibility.

Every generation faces its own storms, but some seasons feel especially unsteady. We live in an age of rapid change, moral confusion, cultural division, and spiritual drift. What once seemed firm now feels fragile. Institutions shake. Families fracture. Truth is questioned. Many people feel as though they are floating through life uncertain and afraid of what lies ahead. In times like these, God does not first send new systems or louder voices. He raises up good men. Good men are not perfect men. They are not flawless, fearless, or immune to pressure. But they are anchored - rooted deeply enough that when everything else is moving, they remain steady. Like anchors dropped into solid ground beneath turbulent waters, good men hold their position so others do not drift into destruction. An anchor has one primary purpose, and this is to hold firm when movement would be dangerous. Ships do not need anchors in calm waters; they need them when the winds howl and the waves rage.

Likewise, society needs good men most - not in peaceful seasons - but in times of instability. Anchors do not stop storms. They do not silence the wind or flatten the waves. What they do is prevent the ship from being pushed onto rocks, carried into unknown waters, or torn apart by relentless motion. In the same way, a good man may not be able to change the world overnight, but his presence can keep families intact, communities grounded, and faith alive. A good man is anchored in truth, not trends. He refuses to redefine right and wrong based on convenience, popularity, or pressure. When truth becomes negotiable in culture, he becomes immovable in conviction. Truth is not loud, but it is weighty. And weight is what makes an anchor effective. While others shift with public opinion, a good man quietly stands on what is eternal. He does not need to win arguments; his life itself becomes evidence. His words carry authority because they come from a heart that is settled on the truth of God's Word.

When confusion spreads, anchored men bring clarity. When lies multiply, anchored men bring light. When compromise is celebrated, anchored men remind others that faithfulness still matters. Anchored men are men of character. In unstable times, character becomes a lifeline for others. People instinctively search for men whose lives are consistent, dependable, and trustworthy. A good man's character does not collapse under pressure. Storms reveal what foundations cannot be seen in calm weather. Trials expose whether a man is built on sand or anchored to bedrock. When systems fail and leaders fall, men of character become reference points. Their integrity provides reassurance to frightened hearts. Their self-control becomes a refuge in a world addicted to impulse. True character isn't loud or dramatic - it is quietly powerful, revealed in consistent choices, unwavering integrity, and faithfulness when no one is watching. It holds when emotions surge and strengthens when others weaken.

Good men are anchored in responsibility. They do not abandon their posts. They do not flee when pressure mounts or excuse themselves when commitment becomes costly. They understand that responsibility is not a burden - it is a calling. In unstable times, many men retreat. Some disengage emotionally. Others withdraw spiritually. Still others escape into distractions. But anchored men remain present. A good man shows up when it's inconvenient, stands firm when it's uncomfortable, and stays faithful when walking away would be easier because his character, not his comfort, leads the way. A good man anchors his family by his presence, and he anchors his workplace by his work ethic. He anchors his church by his faithfulness, and he anchors his community by his willingness to serve. When he shows up consistently - emotionally, spiritually, and physically - he becomes a steady point in a shifting world. His calm reassures, his integrity guides, and his faith strengthens those around him.

Above all, good men are anchored in faith. Not shallow faith that collapses under disappointment, but deep faith forged through prayer, obedience, and trust in God's sovereignty. A good man is not defined by the absence of storms in his life, but by what holds him steady when those storms rage. While others drift with culture, emotion, and fear, the man of God is secured in something deeper, stronger, and eternal. Faith is the anchor of the soul. It does not remove the waves, but it prevents shipwreck. Faith anchors a man when answers are delayed, when outcomes are uncertain, and when obedience costs more than compromise. An anchored man understands that his security does not come from circumstances, success, or control but from God. Because his confidence is rooted in heaven, he is not easily shaken by the earth. When fear grips others, he remains calm. When panic spreads, he remains prayerful. When despair rises, he remains hopeful. His faith does not deny reality - it overcomes it.

Good men are anchors for others because they are first anchored to God. A good man understands that feelings change, circumstances shift, and people disappoint but through it all God remains faithful. Because his trust is not placed in his own strength, he does not panic when pressure comes. He leans into God when the wind howls and the waters rise. Anchored men are not easily moved. They do not abandon truth when it becomes unpopular, nor do they compromise conviction for comfort. When temptation pulls, faith holds. When adversity presses, faith steadies. When doubt whispers, faith answers with the promises of God. A man anchored in faith leads differently. He speaks with calm when others react in chaos. He walks with humility because he knows his footing comes from God, not pride. His decisions are not driven by fear of loss but by confidence in God's direction. He can wait when patience is required and act boldly when obedience demands courage.

The storms will come but they do not get the final word. A man anchored in faith stands firm, holds fast, and finishes strong, not because the sea is calm, but because his anchor is sure. Heb. 6:19 says "We have this hope as an anchor for the soul, firm and secure." One of the greatest truths about anchors is that they do not just hold the ship in place - they also protect everyone on board. Good men may never fully see the impact of their faithfulness. Children may not realize it until years later. Communities may never applaud it. But countless lives are steadied because one man refused to drift. A good man's stability gives others permission to believe again. His endurance inspires courage in weary hearts. His obedience becomes a boundary against chaos. He may feel unnoticed, but he is essential. The world today needs anchored men, men who will stand when standing is costly, men who will remain when leaving is easier, and men who will hold firm when everything else is shaking.

The absence of good men leaves a void in the world and nature always fills a vacuum. When men withdraw, chaos advances. But when men step forward in godliness, order is restored. This is not a call for louder men, harsher men, or prideful men. This is a call for men of character, men who are anchored in the ways of God. Men who are anchored fear God more than they fear rejection. They choose discipline over self-indulgence, and they understand that their lives preach a sermon whether they speak or not. Now is not the time for retreat. Now is the time to man up and march forward. The world doesn't need men who blend in, it needs men who stand out by their faith, their courage, and their love. Good men are needed like never before to stand with courage, lead with integrity, love with conviction, and be a steady light in a world desperate for truth and strength. God is asking, "Who will go for Me?" May the answer rise up from the hearts of men willing to stand in the gap.

Good families are the product of anchored men, men who become a man by acting like a man. The question to be asked is, "How do men act and how do you judge your performance as a man?" Paul tells us in 1 Cor. 16:13,14 (ESV), "Be watchful, stand firm in the faith, act like men, be strong. Let all that you do be done in love." The Message Bible says, "Keep your eyes open, hold tight to your convictions, give it all you've got, be resolute, and love without stopping." These are your primary duties as a man. Paul says to be a real man you must see more, do more, give more, love more. In other words, a real man does more than what is expected of him. God has called you to man up because you are called to be a leader in your home, at your church, and at your work-place. You are called to shine so bright that you draw people to God. This is your call in life and it's never too late to become the man God called you to be. With God, every day is a fresh start, a new beginning.

Anchored men see more. They're watchful because real men don't live for themselves. There are too many selfish men in the world. Open up your eyes and see more of what's going on around you so you'll be able to consider the needs of others. Phil. 2:4 says, "Do not merely look out for your own personal interests, but also for the interest of others." God told Abraham, "I will bless you, and you will be a blessing" (Gen. 12:2). C.S. Lewis said, "True humility is not thinking less of yourself, it's thinking of yourself less." You are called to spiritually protect your family. You are their guardian so be on your guard at all times. Pray for you family! Speak the Word over them. James 5:16, "The prayer of a righteous man is powerful and effective. It avails much." There is spiritual warfare going on every day. The enemy is like a roaring lion, and he wants to destroy you and your family. Resist the devil and he will flee from you (James 4:7). Never let your wife fight your battles. Man up! Take charge! Fight the enemy!

188 - RANDALL J. BREWER

Anchored men do more. Jesus said in Matt. 5:41, "If anyone forces you to go one mile, go with them two miles." Going the second mile is not weakness; it is spiritual strength. The first mile may be demanded of you by circumstances, authority, or injustice but the second mile is chosen. It is the mile where the heart is revealed. Anyone can endure what they are forced to do, but only a transformed heart will willingly give more than what is required. This act of unexpected generosity reflects the character of Christ, who went far beyond what was required when He carried His cross for us. The second mile is where light shines in dark places, where love speaks louder than words, and where people encounter God through our actions. It declares that we are not driven by obligation but by obedience to a higher kingdom. Jesus calls us to live beyond the minimum, to love beyond convenience, and to serve beyond expectation. The second mile is not about pleasing people - it is about honoring God.

Anchored men give more. Throughout the Bible, we're taught that giving leads to growing. If you want to grow, you have to sow. Prov. 11:24 (MSG), "The world of the generous gets larger and larger; the world of the stingy gets smaller and smaller." If you want your family to love you, love them first. If you want a friend, be a friend. Trust God to help you give more than you think you have to give. God designed generosity to be an expanding force in a person's life. According to this proverb, generosity doesn't just affect what you give - it determines the size of the world you live in. The generous person lives in a widening place, while the stingy person slowly shrinks into limitation. Generosity stretches the heart beyond self-preservation. When you give freely of your time, resources, encouragement, forgiveness, or compassion, you'll begin to see life through God's eyes. Your concerns move beyond "mine" to "ours," and your vision expands from survival to purpose.

A generous heart has room for people, faith, and possibility. Stinginess isn't just about money; it's a mindset rooted in fear and scarcity. The stingy person guards everything - resources, trust, grace - because they believe there won't be enough tomorrow. Over time, this fear-driven posture creates isolation. Relationships narrow. Faith contracts. Joy diminishes. What once felt like protection becomes a prison. In the kingdom of God, increase does not come from hoarding but from releasing. What we cling to tightly often loses its power to bless us. But what we place in God's hands through generosity multiplies. When we give, we are declaring our trust in God's supply rather than our own control. The generous person walks in a growing world, a world of new relationships, new opportunities, deeper influence, and greater joy. God entrusts more to those who prove they are conduits, not containers. Generosity signals spiritual maturity because it reflects confidence in who God is and what He provides.

Anchored men love more. They understand that love is a decision and is not based on how you feel. Show love even when you don't feel like it, when you're having a bad day. Your loved ones need you to love them no matter what type of day you're having. Put your feelings aside and give them the love they deserve. Look at the hands and feet of Jesus - love always leaves a mark. Yes, there will be days when love feels easy - when patience flows, kindness comes naturally, and grace feels light. But there will also be days when you wake up tired, wounded, disappointed, or overwhelmed. On those days, love does not feel natural at all. Yet those are the days when love matters most. Love is not proven when circumstances are favorable. Love is revealed when everything in you wants to withdraw, react, or shut down but you choose to give anyway. Showing love on a bad day is an act of obedience before it is an act of emotion. Feelings come and go, but love rooted in faith stands firm.

When you love even when you don't feel like it, you mirror the heart of God who loved us not because we were lovable, but because He is love. Loving on hard days means choosing restraint instead of retaliation. It means speaking gently when irritation is loud, offering grace when offense feels justified, and extending kindness when you feel empty. It means refusing to let your pain turn into poison. Bad days test whether love lives in your emotions or in your character. Anyone can love when it feels good, but it takes spiritual maturity to love when it costs something. When you choose love on difficult days, you break cycles of anger, bitterness, and division. You stop the spread of hurt instead of multiplying it. You become a living testimony that God's love is not conditional but powerful and intentional. Love given on a bad day is seed planted in hard soil but it still bears fruit. So when you're tired, frustrated, or discouraged, remember that love is not about how you feel, it's about who you are becoming.

A real man is not measured by how much he takes, but by how much he carries. Not by how loudly he speaks, but by how deeply he sees. True manhood is not found in comfort, dominance, or applause - it is revealed in vision, action, sacrifice, and love. A boy looks only at what is in front of him, man learns to see beyond the moment. A real man sees the needs others overlook, the consequences others ignore, and the future others fail to prepare for. He sees his family not just as they are, but as they can become. He sees his calling not as a title, but as a responsibility. He sees people not as obstacles or tools, but as souls entrusted to his care. Spiritual sight is maturity. When a man begins to see more, he begins to lead instead of reacting. He knows that vision without action is illusion. A real man does not wait to be asked to step forward. He does not need perfect conditions or constant motivation. He steps forward because someone must take the initiative and he has decided that someone will be him.

He does more when others make excuses, when the work is unseen, and when the cost is personal. He shows up, he follows through, and he finishes what he starts. Strength is not found in potential - it is revealed in faithful action. A boy asks, "What can I get?" A man asks, "What can I give?" A real man gives his time when it is inconvenient, his strength when he is tired, his wisdom when others are confused. He understands that everything he has - ability, opportunity, influence - was never meant to stop with him. He gives not because he has excess, but because he has purpose. A real man sees more because he has learned wisdom. He does more because he has embraced responsibility. He gives more because he understands purpose.

He loves more because he has encountered God. This is not weakness; this is biblical strength. This is how boys become men; this is how men become leaders. This is how faith becomes legacy. And this is how a real man lives.

| 17 |

"A NEW STANDARD"

The pursuit of manhood is not a casual walk in the park. On the contrary, it is a demanding journey marked by dangers, toils, and snares. Every man who sets his heart on becoming who God created him to be will face resistance. There will be opposition from the world, from others, and often from within himself. This is not a sign that he is on the wrong path, it is proof that he is on the right one. True manhood is forged under pressure. Comfort does not produce strength; ease does not develop courage. The road to maturity requires a man to man up, to confront fear, shoulder responsibility, and endure hardship without surrendering his integrity. Along the way, temptations lie in wait—shortcuts that promise relief but steal purpose, distractions that dull conviction, and compromises that weaken the soul. This is why God repeatedly calls men to be courageous and strong. Is. 40:29 says, "He gives power to the weak, and to those who have no might He increases strength."

God's strength is real, available, and sufficient. He will give you strength if you'll trust Him in your time of weakness. You can be a mighty man of valor who is "strong in the Lord and in the power of His might" (Eph. 6:10). Courage is not the absence of fear; it is the resolve to move forward in obedience despite fear. Strength is not merely physical - it is moral, spiritual, and emotional firmness anchored in truth. A strong man stands when others retreat. A courageous man remains faithful when the cost is high. The enemy targets men because he knows that when a man stands firm, families are secure and strengthened, communities are stabilized, and future generations are protected. Weak men create chaos; strong men create order. Passive men leave voids; courageous men fill them with leadership and love. Manhood demands vigilance. Snares are subtle. They often appear harmless at first—unchecked anger, secret sin, spiritual laziness, or the gradual lowering of standards.

Without courage, a man drifts. Without strength, he folds. But with both, he endures. God never promised the path would be easy, but He did promise His presence. Strength grows when a man learns to rely on God rather than his own ability. Courage deepens when he understands that obedience matters more than approval. The man who walks with God may stumble, but he will not be defeated. Walking with God does not mean a man never slips, never falters, or never feels the weight of weakness. It means that when his foot catches on the stone, he does not fall alone. Heaven is near to the man who walks in step with the Lord. Stumbling is part of the human journey. Even the righteous face moments of misjudgment, exhaustion, and fear. But defeat is not determined by a stumble - it is determined by whether a man stays down. The man who walks with God rises again because his strength does not come from his own resolve, but from the hand that upholds him.

God does not abandon His sons when they misstep. He steadies them. He corrects them. He strengthens them. What could have ended another man becomes a lesson, a refinement, and a testimony. The enemy may celebrate the stumble, but heaven prepares the comeback. A man walking with God learns the sacred truth that falling is temporary, but faith is permanent. The ground may shake beneath him, but the foundation beneath his feet is unmovable. Each time he rises, he rises wiser. Each time he endures, his roots grow deeper. The man who walks with God does not fear stumbling, because he knows who is walking beside him. He knows that grace will lift him, mercy will restore him, and truth will realign his steps. His journey is not defined by his failures, but by the faithfulness of the One who leads him. He may stumble but he will not be defeated. God is still with him, and the path ahead still leads to victory. So press on. Embrace the hardship. Reject the shortcuts. Stand your ground.

The pursuit of manhood is costly, but the reward is a life of purpose, honor, and unshakable faith. Be courageous and strong because your calling demands it. When you man up, you inspire others to be the same way. Live your life in such a way that you can be an example that others can follow. 1 Cor. 11:1, "Follow my example as I follow the example of Christ." Paul did not claim perfection, nor did he ask to be followed for his own sake. Instead, his life functioned as a living arrow, pointing toward Jesus. The value of any spiritual example is measured by how clearly it reflects Christ. To follow Christ means to walk in humility, obedience, sacrifice, and love. Paul had learned this through hardship, persecution, discipline, and devotion. His faith was not theoretical - it was tested in real life. That is why his example carried weight. When others looked at Paul, they could see Christ's character forming within him. Remember, manhood and Christlikeness are synonymous terms - they mean the same thing.

Don't direct your family, lead your family. Don't talk the talk, walk the walk. Families don't need more commands shouted from the sidelines. They need a leader who walks ahead. Directing is easy. Anyone can point, instruct, criticize, or correct. But leading costs something. It requires character, consistency, and courage. A man who only directs says, "Go there." A man who leads says, "Follow me." Be a model they can follow. What you model, you promote. Set the example for them. Live a life that lines up with all the scriptures. Ps. 112:1,2, "How joyful are those who fear and delight in obeying His commands. Their children will be successful everywhere." Your spiritual health affects the spiritual health of your family. Children have never been good at listening to their parents, but they have never failed to imitate them. Your family will only be as strong as you are so man up and take the responsibility to prepare your family for life. If you don't, the world will dictate to them how to live.

Leadership begins with example. Children and spouses don't primarily learn from what you say, they learn from what you do. They watch how you handle pressure. They observe how you speak when we're tired. They notice whether our faith is real on Monday, not just on Sunday. You can tell your family to pray but if they never see you pray, your words carry no weight. You can tell them to be kind but if anger leads your home, kindness will never follow. You can tell them to trust God but if fear rules your decisions, faith will never grow. Lead from the front. Spiritual leadership means going first. Be the first to apologize, the first to forgive, the first to pray, the first to sacrifice, the first to stand strong when life gets hard. When storms come - and they will - your family will not remember your instructions. They will remember your example. Don't be a signpost pointing in the right direction. Be the path they can walk on. The strongest legacy a leader leaves is not advice spoken but a life faithfully lived.

The key to victory is preparation - it doesn't just happen. Deut. 6:6,7, "And these words which I command you today shall be in your heart; you shall teach them diligently to your children and shall talk of them when you sit in your house, when you walk by the way, when you lie down, and when you rise up." Read the Bible with your family. Go to church together. Get them plugged into some ministry in the kingdom of God. Do it believing God will honor your efforts. Stu Weber said, "The measure of a man is the spiritual and emotional health of his family." The spiritual health of a family reflects whether a man walks humbly with God. When a man seeks the Lord and lives by conviction rather than convenience, his home is nourished. Faith becomes more than words; it becomes an atmosphere. His children learn what it means to trust God not because they are told, but because they see it lived out. His spouse finds strength in knowing she is partnered with a man who leads by example, not domination.

In the Garden of Eden, God gave Adam three levels of responsibility. He gave him a will to obey, a will greater than his own. He gave him a work to do. Adam was to follow God's example to create and cultivate. Finally, God gave man a woman to love, a companion for intimacy and fellowship as they followed God together. Unfortunately, Adam was a man who didn't become a real man. He chose a conventional manhood based on personal instinct, human reason, and human reaction. Adam had a selfish perspective. He had no eternal value, and he only lived for himself. Before the fall man had work and relationship. The fall caused man to walk in shame and blame. Today millions of men follow the pattern set by Adam. They become passive and drift away from responsibility, authority, and leadership. It is not marked by loud rebellion, but by quiet surrender. They turn the leadership of their families over to their wives. They wimp out even though God has "hard wired" every man to create and cultivate.

Adam did not fall because he lacked strength. He fell because he refused responsibility. When the serpent spoke, Adam was present but he remained silent. When deception unfolded, Adam was near but disengaged. When sin entered the world, Adam did not intervene - he stood down. God had entrusted him with the garden and the covering of his family, yet he stood by while truth was challenged and order was violated. Sad to say, this pattern did not die with Adam. It multiplied. Today, men stand silently while their homes weaken. They retreat while culture redefines truth. They disengage while marriages fracture and children grow without guidance. Like Adam, they are present but passive. Passivity is not harmless. It is rebellion disguised as comfort. When a man rejects responsibility and refuses leadership, confusion rises. When he abandons courage, compromise takes its place. Passivity is not neutrality; it is a decision to surrender ground God intended a man to guard.

God never called men to be spectators. He called them to be keepers. A man was designed to stand watch, to speak truth, to confront evil, and to bear weight. Responsibility is not a burden - it is a calling. Strength is not dominance - it is obedience. Leadership is not control - it is sacrificial presence. The tragedy of Adam is not just that he sinned, it's that he failed to man up and stand strong against the enemy. He also failed to create and cultivate, two acts of courage given to Adam as the core essence, responsibility, and purpose of his masculinity. Men have the responsibility to create or fix something or fulfill a vision God placed in their heart. Men need to have the attitude of Isaiah who said, "Here I am. Send me" (Is.6:8). God has never called men to sit on the sidelines. From the beginning, the Lord placed responsibility in the hands of men to create, cultivate, protect, and complete what He has entrusted to them. When God places a vision in a man's heart, it is not a suggestion. It is a summons.

Many men feel the stirring of God within them - a burden to build something, to fix what is broken, to lead where others hesitate. Yet too often that vision remains dormant, buried beneath fear, comfort, excuses, or the opinions of others. But heaven does not reward hesitation. Vision demands movement. Every great work of God begins when a man decides that obedience matters more than convenience. Noah stepped up and built an ark when there was no rain. Nehemiah stepped out and rebuilt walls while surrounded by opposition. David stepped forward when others stepped back. None of them waited until conditions were perfect - they moved because God spoke. God does not place visions in men's hearts to frustrate them. He does it to activate them. Stepping up means owning the call - no longer blaming circumstances, upbringing, or past failures. Stepping out means taking the first step even when the path is unclear. Faith is not the absence of fear; it is the refusal to be ruled by it.

The kingdom of God advances when men man up and start walking in obedience. It is your assignment to step up and step out, to trust that the God who placed the vision in your heart will supply the strength to finish it. Yes, there will be roadblocks that will try to hinder you from fulfilling God's mandate for your life, things such as passivity, mediocrity, insignificance, cynicism, doubt, and a lack of courage. But real men reject all these roadblocks and navigate around those challenges and obstacles that stand in his way. Be a man and rise up above the reality of the human condition knowing that God has a specific plan for your life. God sees the potential for greatness that is inside. Allow Him daily to put you on the potter's wheel and you'll become the man He desires you to be. Take steps of action that really count. Albert Einstein said, "Not everything that can be counted counts, and not everything that counts can be counted." Character and development are what counts.

Ask God to give you "true grit" which means "grace plus reliance on God equals internal toughness." 2 Cor. 12:9, "My grace is sufficient for you, for My strength is made perfect in weakness." William Booth said, "The greatness of a man is in direct proportion to the measure of his surrender." Man up and tell God you need help to be a good man. Man up and take courageous steps to become the man God wants you to be. Thankfully, when Adam fell God didn't give up on His plan for man. God sends a new Adam. The Bible describes Jesus as the second Adam in 1 Cor. 15:45-47. Jesus set the pattern for how life was to be lived. He fulfilled the responsibilities of the first Adam. Every man will walk in the shadow of one of these two Adam's. They'll walk in the darkness of the first Adam or the light of the second Adam. John 10:10 says God wants you to experience paradise on earth so he sent a new standard to live by. Jesus is the model you are to follow. He is the example of authentic manhood.

Real men reject passivity. Adam was passive in the garden, but Jesus rejected passivity. From the moment He stepped into public ministry, He demonstrated that the Kingdom of God does not advance through silence, complacency, or spiritual indifference. Jesus confronted evil, challenged religious hypocrisy, corrected error, and called people to decisive action. He did not ignore sin in the name of peace. He did not remain silent to preserve comfort. When truth was at stake, Jesus spoke clearly, boldly, and without compromise. He overturned tables in the temple, rebuked the Pharisees for their hypocrisy, and corrected His own disciples when fear or misunderstanding crept in. His love was not weak; it was courageous. Jesus rejected the idea that righteousness is passive. He taught that light must shine, salt must preserve, and a city on a hill cannot be hidden. Faith was never meant to be quiet agreement but was meant to be active obedience. Everything God tells you to do requires movement.

Even in suffering, Jesus was not passive. He willingly laid down His life, but He did so with purpose and resolve. He endured the cross not because He lacked power, but because He was fulfilling the will of the Father. Submission to God is not passivity; it is strength under control. Jesus calls His followers to the same posture. He does not invite believers to watch from a distance, remain silent in the face of injustice, or drift through life spiritually disengaged. He calls us to stand, speak, serve, and act. To follow Jesus is to resist apathy, confront fear, and live with intentional obedience. Passivity allows darkness to grow unchecked. Jesus confronted it head-on with truth, love, and authority. And He still calls men today to do the same. Faith that truly follows Christ is never passive - it is active, obedient, and alive. Biblical faith is not a quiet agreement with truth; it is a courageous response to truth. It does not sit still while the world moves in the opposite direction. Faith moves, acts, follows, and obeys.

Many people confuse faith with belief alone. They say, "I believe in Christ," yet their lives remain unchanged. But faith that follows Christ is not content with mental assent. It steps out of the boat. It leaves the nets behind. It takes up the cross and walks the narrow road. Faith is proven not by what you say, but by what you do when obedience costs you something. Jesus never called anyone to passive faith. His invitation was always, "Follow Me." Following requires movement. It demands surrender. It requires leaving comfort, familiarity, and control. Faith that follows Christ listens for His voice and responds even when the path is uncertain, even when the outcome is unseen. Passive faith watches from a distance. Active faith will man up and draw near. Passive faith waits for conditions to improve. Active faith trusts God in the storm. Passive faith agrees with scripture. Active faith lives it out daily at work, at home, in private, and in public. This is obedient faith, anchored in the character and promises of God.

Men are passive because they wimp out. The army of Israel feared Goliath, but David ran toward the giant. Elijah faced down the prophets of Baal on Mt. Carmel but wimped out when threatened by Jezebel. Jonah ran away from Ninevah and Peter denied Jesus three times. Men who are passive are uncomfortable doing what they have to do. They lack courage believing it's easier to be passive and do nothing. Men use passivity as a strategy. They think if they ignore a problem maybe it will go away. They don't want to get involved. As men we wimp out too much. We take the easy way out. When you are passive, you put yourself in a position to fail. Consider Paul who got stoned, got up, and walked back into the city from which he came. Consider Jesus Who went to Jerusalem knowing that torture and death awaited Him. Follow their example. Man up and declare war on passivity. Reject comfort over challenge, rise with courage, and take full responsibility to become the man you were created to be.

| 18 |

"SIN NO MORE"

If you want to be a man - a real man - then the issue of sin must be dealt with. Biblical manhood demands confrontation, and it starts with the sin that lives within. Willful and habitual sin will blemish a walk of holiness and will derail your efforts to be a man of God. You cannot call yourself a man while bowing to what destroys your integrity, poisons your marriage, weakens your leadership, and silences your spiritual authority. Every man will fight battles, and the greatest battle is not against the world, the devil, or circumstances - it is against the sin within. Real men don't negotiate with sin. They confront it and then they kill it. This is why you must have a deep, deep desire to get sin out of your life. Sin is not merely a moral failure - it is a spiritual force that seeks dominion. Scripture does not treat sin as a minor inconvenience but as a master that demands obedience. Jesus Himself said, "Whoever commits sin is a slave to sin" (John 8:34). Slaves do not lead with authority, nor do they build lasting legacies.

Manhood is not proven by dominance over others, but by dominion over oneself. It is not proven by perfection, but by repentance. It is not proven by image, but by integrity. Develop in your heart a wholesome dread of hurting and displeasing God. You need to love what God loves and hate what God hates. The "fear of the Lord" means to love God and hate sin. It's a fact, sin will always take you farther than you plan to go, keep you longer than you plan to stay, cost you more than you plan to pay. That's the reality of life. No one plans to end up bound, broken, or distant from God. The first step is usually small - a lustful look, a seducing word, a moment of compromise. But sin is never content with a single step. What begins as curiosity becomes habit. What begins as habit becomes captivity. Sin is progressive by nature because once it is tolerated it never remains satisfied but continually demands more ground, deeper control, and greater surrender of the heart.

At first, you think you can leave whenever you want. But sin dulls discernment and weakens resolve. It numbs conviction and reshapes conscience. The longer you remain, the harder it becomes to recognize how far you've drifted. Days turn into years. What was once optional becomes obligatory. Chains form quietly but they hold firmly. Sin always demands payment, and the price is never revealed upfront. It costs peace. It costs integrity. It costs relationships. It costs spiritual authority. Often, it costs joy, credibility, and influence. In some cases, it costs a legacy. Sin promises pleasure but pays in loss. It never overdelivers, it only overcharges. The greatest danger of sin is not just what it does to you but what it distances you from. Sin separates you from the nearness of God, the clarity of truth, and the power of obedience. It clouds hearing, weakens prayer, and steals boldness. A man may still belong to God, but sin keeps him from walking with Him.

A wise man sees the end from the beginning. He sees the consequences of his actions. He knows that what you sow is what you will reap. Prov. 19:20, "Listen to counsel and receive instruction, that you may be wise in your latter days." The Hebrew word for "latter days" refers to "that which comes after." The wisdom of God is to show you the consequences that come after you sin while the wisdom of the world is to appeal to the flesh in the here and now. The enemy of your soul has never changed his strategy, only his packaging. From the beginning, the devil has worked tirelessly to control what you *see*. He knows that if he can shape your vision, he can influence your desires, and if he can influence your desires, he can guide your decisions. That is why he always presents sin through the narrow lens of immediate pleasures while carefully hiding the long shadow of future consequences. Prov. 3:11 says, "And you mourn at last - that which comes after - when your flesh and your body are consumed."

Sin is never introduced honestly. It never arrives announcing its cost. It never discloses the wreckage it leaves behind. Instead, it comes dressed in charm, convenience, and justification. The devil wants you to see the thrill, not the trap. He wants you to feel the sweetness, not the sickness that follows. He wants you focused on the moment, never the aftermath. The enemy knows that if you saw sin clearly - if you saw the broken homes, the crushed consciences, the lost integrity, the damaged faith, the spiritual numbness, the sleepless nights, the regret, the shame, the separation, the grief - you would run from it. So he blurs the future and magnifies the present. He floods your mind with promises of satisfaction while muting the voice that warns, "This will cost you more than you think." But sin never stays where you invited it. It always asks for more ground. What begins as a suggestion becomes a habit. What starts as curiosity becomes bondage. What feels like freedom slowly tightens into chains.

The devil never tells you that the pleasure you borrow today will demand payment tomorrow with interest. The tragedy is that sin often feels good at first. That is part of the deception. If it were immediately painful, no one would pursue it. But pleasure without righteousness is poison with a sweet coating. It numbs before it destroys. It entertains before it enslaves. It satisfies the flesh while starving the soul. The enemy wants you to believe that consequences are exaggerated, that warnings are outdated, and that restraint is unnecessary. He whispers that holiness is restrictive and obedience is joyless. Yet he never mentions the peace that obedience brings, the clarity that righteousness produces, or the freedom found in a clean conscience. He wants you to believe that sin offers life, while hiding the truth that it only delivers death - spiritually, emotionally, relationally, and sometimes physically. What makes sin so dangerous is that it clouds discernment. It dulls conviction and it hardens the heart.

Sin distances you from God not in one dramatic step, but through small, repeated compromises. Slowly, prayer becomes quieter. Scripture becomes less compelling. Worship feels distant. And before you realize it, what once grieved you now feels normal. The devil is patient. He does not rush destruction. He is content with gradual decay. He knows that a soul drifting is often more dangerous than a soul openly rebelling, because drifting feels harmless until you look up and realize how far you've gone. If you could see sin from God's perspective - if you could see where it leads instead of how it feels - you would treat temptation differently. You would stop asking, "How does this make me feel right now?" and start asking, "Where will this take me later?" You would value your soul over a moment. You would protect your calling over your cravings. You would choose obedience over impulse. The enemy wants you blind to tomorrow. God wants you anchored in truth today.

Nothing good ever comes from sin. It may promise pleasure for a moment, but it always leaves behind hurt, pain, brokenness, and ultimately death. Sin promises you everything your heart desires, but in the end, it robs you of peace, enslaves your soul, and destroys the very life it claimed to fulfill. Prov. 5:3-5 says, "For the lips of an immoral woman drip honey, and her mouth is smoother than oil. But in the end, she is bitter as wormwood, sharp as a two-edged sword, her feet go down to death, her steps lay hold of hell." Consider also Prov. 23:31,32 that says, "Do not look on the wine when it is red, when it sparkles in the cup, when it swirls around smoothly. "At the last it bites like a serpent, and stings like a viper." When temptation comes, think ahead! Ask yourself, "Where is this heading?" Prov. 5:22,23 says, "His own iniquities entrap the wicked man, and he is caught in the cords of his sin. He shall die for lack of instruction, and in the greatness of his folly he shall go astray."

Always look ahead first! If you can see where your sin is taking you, then you'll refrain from that sin. Don't dabble in sin. What you dabble in today can dominate us tomorrow. When it comes to sin, make no exceptions whatsoever. Jesus said to the woman caught in adultery, "Go and sin no more" (John 8:11). Man up and do the same. Sin is not a harmless habit, a private weakness, or a minor flaw in character. Sin is deadly. It destroys slowly at first, quietly convincing the soul that compromise is manageable until the damage is done. Scripture never treats sin lightly, and neither should you. Jesus said in Matt. 5:29, "And if your right eye causes you to sin, pluck it out and cast it from you." In other words, don't cut back from sin, cut it off completely. Jesus was teaching that sin is so destructive, so dangerous to the soul, that no sacrifice is too great to remove it. If something leads you into sin - no matter how precious, convenient, or familiar - it must be dealt with decisively.

Understand that every day you are in a battle with the flesh and sensual desires. Sin promises to satisfy but it never does. Instead, it creates a desire for more. One drink of alcohol, one cigarette, one candy bar, one look at a porno site always creates a desire for more. It creates an addiction. A company that made potato chips had a commercial that said, "You can never eat just one." What they didn't tell you is the way the chips were salted created an appetite for more. Likewise, sin never satisfies. It always leads to more sin. Sin always promises pleasure but delivers bondage. It dulls spiritual sensitivity, hardens the heart, and weakens moral resolve. What begins as a glance becomes a fixation. What begins as a thought becomes an action. What begins as an action becomes a chain. Left unchecked, sin does not remain contained - it spreads, corrupts, and ultimately kills. Jesus' command to "cut it off" demands urgency, courage, and resolve. Delay is dangerous. Tolerance is lethal.

Many men excuse the wrongs they do reasoning they don't commit "big" sins. They don't rob banks or commit murder. But what about that "little white lie" you told your neighbor? Or the time you murmured and complained about what your wife made for dinner. Or the time you gossiped and said, "Did you hear what so-and-so did?" Song of Solomon 2:15 says, "It's the little foxes that spoil the vine." A little sin here and a little sin there will eventually make you a slave to sin. Most damage in the Christian life does not begin with a dramatic fall - it begins quietly. Rarely does the vine die overnight. It is the small, unnoticed intruders that slip in and slowly destroy what God is growing. In Song of Solomon, the vineyard is flourishing. The blossoms are out. Growth is happening. Yet the warning is clear. It's the little foxes that threaten everything. This is a powerful picture of small sins, tolerated habits, and overlooked compromises that quietly devastate spiritual fruitfulness.

When God is moving in your life - when prayer deepens, faith grows, ministry expands - the enemy doesn't always send a storm. Sometimes he sends a fox. Little foxes are dangerous because they appear harmless. After all, they're not lions and neither do they roar. They don't look dangerous because they don't destroy the crops immediately. Foxes don't usually eat the grapes first. They chew the roots which weaken the vine and undermine stability. Little sins often show up as unchecked attitudes such as pride, bitterness, and jealousy. They appear subtle and low-key like small compromises in integrity, neglected prayer, casual obedience, and entertained temptations. The fruit may still look good for a while, but the roots are dying. Eventually, what once thrived begins to wither. Little sins thrive when devotion becomes routine, accountability is absent, conviction is delayed, and repentance is postponed. Neglect always gives permission for the little foxes to enter the vineyard of your life.

Don't play with fire. James 3:5, "A tiny spark can set a great forest on fire." Little sins turn into big sins. You'll end up doing things you never imagined you would do. One marijuana cigarette often leads to an addiction to heroin or cocaine. One look at a porno site often leads to adultery and a failed marriage. David looked at Bathsheba, slept with her, and his life was never the same until the day he died. It's the little foxes that spoil the vine. If you play with fire, you will get burned. Don't flirt with somebody you're not married to. Flirting with a young woman can lead to a relationship that will destroy your marriage, your family, your life. Prov. 7:26,27, "And all who were slain by her were strong men. Her house is the way to hell, descending to the chambers of death." The consequence of sin is like those movies where a monster comes out of a beautiful woman. Don't dabble in sin! It will destroy your life! Prov. 24:20 (NLT) says, "For evil people have no future; the light of the wicked will be snuffed out."

Fire is one of the most fascinating forces God placed in the world. It can warm a home, cook food, and provide light in the darkness. Yet the very same fire - if mishandled - can destroy everything in its path. Fire is never neutral. It either serves you or consumes you. Sin works the same way. No one intends for fire to get out of control. No one plans for devastation. Forest fires don't begin as roaring infernos - they begin as sparks. A careless match. A neglected flame. A moment of inattention. And once it spreads, no amount of regret can undo the damage. One of the greatest lies believers tell themselves is that some sins are harmless. We label them "small," "manageable," or "private." We convince ourselves that as long as we don't cross certain lines, we're safe. But fire doesn't care how small it starts. Sin rarely storms the gates of your life. It slips through cracks. It whispers instead of shouts. It disguises itself as curiosity, stress relief, entitlement, or personal freedom.

Notice that the Bible never warns us about large sparks. It warns us about tiny ones because those are the most dangerous. They go unnoticed. They are ignored. They are justified. And by the time they are seen for what they truly are, the forest is already burning. A single spark doesn't look threatening. It looks manageable. But sparks spread quickly when there is fuel. A thought becomes a habit, and a small compromise becomes a lifestyle. A hidden sin becomes public disgrace, and a neglected conviction becomes a hardened heart. Forests don't burn all at once. They burn tree by tree. Conviction by conviction. Relationship by relationship. Prayer by prayer. The damage happens slowly until suddenly it's everywhere. Sin never remains isolated. It bleeds into attitudes, words, decisions, and priorities. It robs you of clarity, dulls your spiritual senses, and erodes your authority. And while grace forgives, the scars of burned ground often remain. Some fires don't just burn trees, they burn destinies.

Sin grows and if not removed, little sins grow into big sins. An adulterous affair always begins with a lustful glance in the wrong direction. We all know that sin does not leave on its own. This means you are responsible for getting sin out of your life. You start by being prepared for the temptation to sin when it comes. Know the circumstances under which you are most likely to commit a particular sin. Let's say you criticize your boss when you sit with your co-workers at lunch break. Be aware of this and sit somewhere else. Don't risk sinning for the sake of being "one of the guys." Perhaps you've begun to flirt with the young female cashier at the gas station. Don't destroy your life and family because you can't control your flesh. Start getting gas at a different station. Keep the sin and the circumstances ever before you. Do not ignore the sin! Focus on it! Zero in on it! Know the circumstances where you're most likely to sin. If you'll do that, you'll be ready for it and you'll be able to prevent yourself from sinning.

Sin promises pleasure but leaves ashes. Holiness demands discipline but preserves life. You cannot play with fire and remain unchanged. You cannot flirt with sin and escape its cost. You cannot hold a spark and expect your forest to survive. God's call to holiness is not a call to deprivation - it is a call to preservation. He wants to protect your purpose, your witness, your family, and your future. The safest fire is the one that never starts. Spiritual maturity is not proven by how much temptation you can withstand - it's proven by how quickly you respond when temptation appears. The longer a spark burns, the harder it is to extinguish. Do not negotiate with what God has already judged. Do not manage what God has called you to kill. Do not delay repentance while the flame is still small. Run to God and put the fire out early. Confess quickly. Repent thoroughly. Cut off access. Change patterns. Invite accountability. Fill your life with what deprives sin of oxygen - truth, prayer, obedience, and reverence for God.

Most spiritual failures do not come from rebellion; they come from proximity. People don't fall because they hate God. They fall because they stood too close to temptation for too long. They flirted with what they should have fled. They entertained what should have been extinguished. They treated holiness casually and temptation confidently. God never instructs His people to see how close they can get to sin without consequences. He commands us to flee, cut off, put to death, and separate. These are not gentle words. They are urgent commands because the danger is real. God does not warn us because He is controlling - He warns us because He is loving. James is not trying to condemn believers; he is trying to protect them. God sees what we cannot see. He knows how quickly sparks spread. He understands the cost of cleanup after the fire has passed. Restoration is possible, but prevention is far better. Yes, grace will forgive you, but wisdom will keep you from lighting the match.

| 19 |

"TOUR OF DUTY"

The first step in the journey to manhood is the step of surrender. A man reaches his greatest strength not when he grips life tighter, but when he releases control into God's hands. Surrender is not frailty or weakness - it is trust. It means laying down pride, self-reliance, and fear, and choosing obedience over ego. When a man yields his plans, desires, and direction to God, he gains clarity, purpose, and peace that self-control can never produce. True leadership begins on the knees, and true freedom is found when God is in control. Be like Jesus who said, "Not my will but Your will be done" (Luke 22:42). True transformation doesn't begin with asking God to change your circumstances - it begins with you ask Him to change you. When you humble yourself before Him and surrender your pride, habits, and desires, you invite God to shape your heart according to His original design. He is not trying to make you into someone else, but into the person He created you to be from the beginning.

When you ask God to change you, you give Him permission to refine your character, renew your mind, and align your life with His purpose. Real growth happens when you say in prayer, "Lord, change me into the person You created me to be." Today is the day to do it. Now is the time to man up, to step up, and embrace God's call on your life. Not tomorrow. Not when life gets easier. Not when fear loosens its grip. Now is the moment God is calling men to rise. For too long, too many men have stood on the sidelines waiting, hesitating, excusing delay with comfort or fear. But heaven is not asking for excuses. Heaven is calling for men of courage, men who will stand up, step forward, and take responsibility for the life God has entrusted to them. Biblical manhood is not about ego - it is about obedience. It is humility before God, and boldness in the face of adversity. A man who has truly "manned up" has settled the question of lordship in his heart. God is in charge, no matter what the cost may be.

Stepping up means accepting responsibility instead of running from it. It means leading when it would be easier to follow, standing when others bow, and speaking truth when silence feels safer. God is not looking for perfect men - He is looking for available men. Every generation rises or falls on the backs of men who either answered God's call or ignored it. Your family, your church, your community, and your generation need men who will pray when it's hard, lead when it's lonely, and remain faithful when no one is applauding. God's call on your life is not an accident. You were not born in the wrong era, to the wrong family, or with the wrong gifts. You were crafted by God for such a time as this. Your life matters and the enemy fears men who know who they are in God. That's why he works so hard to keep you distracted, passive, or discouraged. But today, God is stirring something deep within you. He is calling out the warrior, the leader, the servant, the man of faith He designed you to be.

The time for half-hearted faith is over. The time for excuses has passed. The world does not need softer men - it needs strong men with surrendered hearts. It needs men who are loyal, men who love God and seek to please Him in all their thoughts and actions. A man's loyalty is the truest measure of his love. He may speak many words, make many promises, and express many intentions but what he remains loyal to reveals what truly owns his heart. Love is not proven by emotion alone; it is proven by allegiance. A man will protect what he loves. He will sacrifice for what he loves. He will stay committed to what he loves even when it costs him comfort, convenience, or applause. Where a man invests his time, his strength, and his attention, that is where his loyalty lies. Scripture reminds us that "where your treasure is, there your heart will be also" (Matt. 6:21). A man's treasure is not only his money - it is his energy, his focus, and his perseverance. These never lie.

1 Cor. 16:13,14 says, "Watch, stand fast in the faith, be brave, be strong. Let all that you do be done with love." The Message Bible says, "Keep your eyes open, hold tight to your convictions, give it all you've got, be resolute, and love without stopping." NIV, "Be on your guard; stand firm in the faith; be courageous; be strong. Do everything in love." How do you

step up and act like a man? Be watchful of what's going on around you. Stand firm in the faith. Be strong, bear the weight of leadership. Act like men! Let all you do be done in love. That's where the power is. Men were born to be great. Recognition is not greatness. Greatness is faithfulness and doing what is right with dignity and courage. Greatness is facing those things that are principled and right over a long period of time. Greatness is to never walk away from responsibility. God is going to call you to do great things. Do your duty with excellence and honor, knowing that obedience in every role shapes your character and fulfills a greater purpose.

God has never called ordinary people to live ordinary lives. From the beginning, He has chosen men to carry out extraordinary purposes. The call of God is not small, timid, or accidental - it is intentional, weighty, and filled with eternal significance. When God calls you, He is inviting you into something far greater than personal comfort or recognition. He is calling you to a tour of duty. Great things rarely begin with great stages. They begin with obedience in obscurity. Moses tended sheep before he confronted Pharaoh. David watched over his father's flock before he faced Goliath. Nehemiah served faithfully as a cupbearer before rebuilding a broken city. God often assigns small responsibilities before revealing larger destinies, not because He doubts your ability, but because He is shaping your character. Your assignment may not look glorious. It may feel unnoticed, inconvenient, or beneath your expectations. But heaven measures greatness differently than the world.

Faithfulness is the currency of the Kingdom. God is not looking for those who seek applause - He is looking for those who
will do their duty whether anyone is watching or not. When
you honor your assignment, you honor the One who gave it.
Obedience in the present unlocks promotion in the future. You
do not choose the timing, the size, or the visibility of your calling - you choose faithfulness. And faithfulness positions you
for greater responsibility. Do not despise the place where God
has planted you. Do not abandon your post because it feels
slow or silent. Stay alert. Stay committed. Stay obedient. God
sees every act of faith, every unseen sacrifice, every quiet "yes"
spoken in the dark. The same God who calls you to duty is
the God who elevates at the appointed time. Great things are
coming but they are entrusted only to those who prove faithful
with what is in their hands right now. Stand firm. Serve well.
Do your duty. Your obedience today is preparing you for God's
greater tomorrow.

All men all called to be soldiers in the army of the Lord, and
your tour of duty began on the day you arrived on this planet
and ends when you leave. You've got a job to do. You're not
here to see how many toys you can buy or how many rounds of
golf you can play. 2 Tim. 2:4 says, "No one engaged in warfare
entangles himself with the affairs of this life." The word "en-
tangle" means to become involved in an activity to the point
of interference with other activities or objectives. Like a ram
whose horns are caught in the brush, one is entangled when
he is not free to get loose. Samson got entangled with Delilah
and Lot got entangled with Sodom. In the New Testament the
rich young ruler got entangled with money, so much so that he

walked away from the call on his life. Deut. 20:5-8 warns a man not to go to war if there are unsettled affairs in his life. The battle is serious, and a true soldier must stay focused on the mission, refusing to be distracted or entangled by the cares of business and the pull of worldly affairs.

A soldier in the fight needs to concentrate on the task of doing the Lord's work and must avoid all preoccupation with the daily affairs of life in order to be free to obey without hesitation the orders of the commander-in-chief. You are called to be in the world but not to be entangled by it. This means if you truly want to get serious about being a man and serving God, you must accept the uncomfortable truth that there will be times when you can't do what other people do. For example, Moses refused to be called the son of Pharaoh's daughter, choosing rathe to suffer affliction with the people of God than to enjoy the passing pleasures of sin (Heb. 11:24,25). Soldiers must avoid anything that hampers their effectiveness in battle. They are to be so consumed with their duties that they are oblivious to the enticement of this world and the non-essentials of life. The active service for Christ must always occupy the prominent place in your heart while the things of this life are kept in the background.

All men are called, delivered, and set free so they can be in active service to the Lord and will always be on the front lines of battle whether they realize it or not. This means the active soldier must forever be on guard against becoming so involved in such matters that he no longer feels free to give himself fully to the call of Christian service. Service to God always brings restriction. A child can run anywhere, say anything, and chase every impulse. A man cannot. A man lives with purpose, discipline, and direction. The moment you decide to serve God wholeheartedly, your freedom changes. Others may indulge, compromise, laugh it off, or go along with the crowd. You won't always have that luxury. Your calling demands restraint. Your integrity demands boundaries. Your future demands sacrifice. There will be conversations you walk away from. Places you no longer go. Relationships you leave behind. If you want to be serious about God, understand that separation is part of the assignment.

All soldiers know that serving God as a man is hazardous duty and one must be able to endure hardship and be strong in the grace that is in Christ Jesus (2 Tim. 2:1-3). Scripture never presents the call of Christ as safe, comfortable, or convenient. It is a summons to battle, endurance, and sacrifice. This is not language of leisure. It is the language of war. The strength required for this mission does not come from pride or bravado - it comes from dependence on God alone. Grace is not weakness; grace is divine power supplied to men who refuse to quit. A man who serves God must learn to draw strength daily from Christ, because the assignment will demand more than human endurance can provide. Hardship is not an accident; it is part of the call. Difficulty is not a sign that you are off course - it is often proof that you are right where God wants you. Serving God means facing resistance, misunderstanding, rejection, spiritual opposition, and seasons of loneliness. This is why all men need to man up!

God is not surprised by the cost. He designed the mission knowing the price and He calls men who are willing to pay it. Soldiers find out early on that they're not called to a life of ease and comfort. All men are to be tough warriors and there is no room for passive wimps and whining cry-babies in the army of the Lord. A soldier fights in all conditions. They'll fight in the rain, snow, and 120-degree heat. They'll crawl in the mud, run in a storm, eat out of a can, sleep under the stars, carry heavy equipment, and go long hours without rest or sleep. They train hard and will do whatever it takes to win and overcome. They will go anywhere, at any time, at any cost. Active service calls for rigorous self-discipline and unquestioning obedience for a soldier is always on duty and needs to be alert around the clock. Total commitment is necessary to be a good soldier, and his training is designed to make him obey the word of command. A soldier is conditioned to obedience and puts priority on the task at hand.

The Bible compares the servant of God to a soldier. Soldiers do not expect ease; they expect conflict. They train for endurance. They accept sacrifice. They understand that the mission is bigger than personal comfort. A man who serves God will not retreat when the battle gets hard and neither will he abandon his post when the pressure rises. This is hazardous duty, but it is holy duty. Our generation does not need softer men; it needs strong men who are anchored in grace. It needs men who can endure hardship without becoming bitter, men who can suffer without surrendering their faith, and men who can stand when others fall away. God is still calling men to this dangerous, demanding, and glorious assignment. If you are serving God and it feels heavy, you are not failing - you are fighting the good fight. Man up and be strong in grace. Endure hardship. Stand your ground. The battle is real, but so is the reward. A good soldier does not quit the war because it is dangerous. He was enlisted for it.

A good soldier must not allow the ordinary affairs of life to become the main object of his existence. This world is not your home. It is a temporary dwelling place and not a permanent residence. We live here as travelers passing through, not settling down. Live with the awareness that this life is short and there is a better world to come. Live your life with the end in mind and you'll stop measuring success by what you accumulate and start measuring it by who you become. Living with eternity in view will give you clarity and courage. You'll endure hardship without despair because you know suffering is temporary. You'll walk in hope even when circumstances are dark, because your future is secure. You'll refuse to compromise your faith for comfort, because comfort here is fleeting, but reward there is eternal. So live with awareness. Wake up each day remembering that you are just passing through. Let heaven shape your priorities. Let eternity guide your decisions. And let hope anchor your soul.

God is not glorified by half-hearted faith or casual obedience. He is honored when men give Him their whole heart, their full strength, and their undivided attention. Scripture shows that wholehearted devotion, marked by hard work and careful attention to God's Word, releases the greatest glory to the Lord. True devotion puts forth great labor which the man of

God works into the fabric of daily life. Hard work in spiritual matters is love expressed through obedience. Just as an athlete trains with discipline or a farmer labors with patience, the devoted man understands that service unto God requires great effort. This effort does not earn salvation, but it reveals devotion. God is glorified when men are willing to sweat spiritually - to resist temptation, to persevere in obedience, and to remain faithful when the path is difficult. Wholehearted devotion says, "I will hold nothing back." And when nothing is held back, God receives the greatest glory. He is honored, His truth is upheld, and His name is magnified.

There is a quiet emptiness that no possession, position, or personal achievement can fill. You can chase success, comfort, and recognition, yet still feel a hollow place within your soul. That emptiness is not a flaw - it is a divine signal. God did not design you to be fulfilled by living for yourself. True satisfaction is found when your life becomes a blessing to someone else. You were created in the image of a giving God. From the beginning, the Lord's nature has been outward-focused - loving, serving, and sacrificing. When you live only to meet your own needs, you work against your own design. But when you step outside yourself to lift another, something sacred happens inside you. Joy rises. Purpose awakens. Fulfillment flows. Scripture reminds us that "it is more blessed to give than to receive" (Acts 20:35). That blessing is not merely material - it is deeply spiritual. When you feed the hungry, encourage the weary, forgive the undeserving, or serve without recognition, your soul aligns with heaven.

Men of honor are always ready and willing to serve, anytime, anywhere. People live like they'll be here forever, but the truth is that your life on this planet is the shortest thing you'll ever do. The longer you live the faster you realize that life is passing you by quickly. Always remember, you were not made for this life, you were made for eternity so live with the end in mind. The reason you feel restless may not be because you lack something - it may be because someone else needs what God placed within you. Your time, your compassion, your wisdom, your strength - these are not just gifts for your benefit; they are answers to someone else's prayer. You will never be fully satisfied until your life becomes an instrument of goodness in the hands of God. So look around. There is a need near you. There is a person waiting for kindness. Step into that moment. Do something good for somebody else - not to be seen, not to be applauded, but to obey the calling written into your soul.

To go on with the Lord and fulfill the call He has for you requires great levels of commitment and dedication. When you put your hand to the plow of service unto the Lord never look back to the fleeting pleasures that this life has to offer. God will call you out of your comfort zone and if you're willing to turn loose of some things you'll quickly find out how better off life will be. Good soldiers go where they're sent and stay where they're stationed. There is a place for you and a service you are to perform. When you turn loose of self will and submit to the will of God then fullness of joy will overwhelm you. If you don't step up and obey, you'll never know what you missed. The children of Israel didn't cross over the Jordan River and died in the wilderness. There are sacrifices to be made and much effort is needed but it will make you feel good and want to get up each morning. Soldiers in the army of the Lord are eager and enthusiastic about advancing the kingdom of God. Let the battle begin!

| 20 |

"YOUR FULL POTENTIAL"

The purpose of every God-fearing man is to whole-heartedly pour their lives into the work God gives them to do with the ability God gives them to do it. Purpose is the reason something exists and potential is the ability to perform the task at hand. When God creates something for a purpose, He puts in it its own potential. This means that potential is a byproduct of purpose. God never creates aimlessly. He never designs without intention. Purpose always comes first, and potential follows as a natural result. The mistake many people make is trying to discover their potential before they understand their calling and purpose. But in God's order, it works the other way around. Purpose precedes potential. You do not receive potential randomly; you receive potential because God has assigned you a reason for existing. The moment God decided your purpose, the reason why you are needed in the world, He determined what you would need to reach your full potential and then graciously give it to you.

God did not create you without placing within you the capacity to do what He called you to do. Your potential is not something you must beg God to give you later - it is something He already placed inside you when He gave you purpose. Think of purpose as the blueprint and potential as the materials. The blueprint determines what materials are necessary. A house requires different materials than a bridge. A bridge requires different materials than a ship. The design determines the supply. Likewise, your God-given purpose determines the potential embedded within you. If God called you to lead, leadership capacity is already present. If God called you to serve, compassion is already planted. If God called you to endure, strength has already been deposited. If God called you to build, creativity and wisdom are already inside you. You may not understand it yet, but the presence of purpose guarantees the existence of potential because God never assigns a calling without also supplying the capacity to carry it out.

One reason people doubt their potential is because potential often remains dormant until purpose places a demand on it. A seed looks insignificant until it is planted. Muscles look weak until resistance is applied. Faith looks small until a trial requires it to grow. God does not always reveal your full potential at once. If He did, you might rely on yourself instead of trusting Him. Instead, He allows purpose-driven pressure to awaken what He already placed inside you. The trial didn't create your strength - it revealed it. The challenge didn't invent your faith - it exposed it. The calling didn't produce your ability - it activated it. What you are facing right now may not be evidence of your limitation - it may be evidence of your full potential being summoned. Many believers live with a mind-set of lack. They say, "I'm not ready," "I'm not gifted," or "I don't have what it takes." But if God has assigned you a purpose, lack is not your problem - alignment and tapping into your full potential is.

Remember, God never assigns purpose without provision and He never gives a calling without the potential to carry it out. It's true, He never demands fruit where He has not planted seed. You may not yet be skilled, but potential precedes skill. You may not yet be confident, but potential precedes confidence. You may not yet be experienced, but potential precedes experience. Growth is simply the process of uncovering what God already placed inside you. Know also that potential remains unused when purpose is ignored. Many people possess enormous potential but live frustrated lives because they resist the very purpose that would activate it. Unfortunately, the graveyard is filled with people who never reached their full potential. Inside of them was dormant ability, untapped power, hidden strength, and reserved energy. Do not be like these people who died without fulfilling their destiny, having never reached their full potential. Your future greatness is trapped in the potential that is inside of you.

Potential does not flourish in disobedience; it flourishes in alignment. When you walk in God's will your potential begins to surface, your gifts start making sense, your passion becomes clearer, and your strength increases. Obedience is the environment where potential thrives. You don't need a new anointing - you need obedience to the calling you already have. You don't need a new gift - you need faithfulness with what God has already given. Your potential is proof that God is not finished with you yet. If you are still breathing, God is still working. The fact that you feel stirred, challenged, or unsettled is evidence that unused potential remains inside you. God never reveals purpose to frustrate you - He reveals it to invite you into growth. Your future is not limited by your past. Your calling is not canceled by your failures. Your potential is not erased by your mistakes. Purpose remains. And because purpose remains, potential remains. Walk in your purpose, and your potential will rise to meet you.

Whatever you've done in the past is no longer your potential and where you're at today is not the end of the journey. Potential is not past tense, it's future tense. Potential is always what you haven't done yet but one day will do. Potential is not a story about what could have been; it's a promise of what can still be. It does not live in yesterday's failures or missed opportunities. Potential lives ahead of you in the work you haven't done yet, the courage you haven't fully exercised, and the obedience you haven't completely walked out. If your potential were past tense, it would already be finished. But it's not. It is future tense - waiting on your faith, your discipline, and your willingness to move forward. Every new day is proof that God is not done with you yet. What remains undone is not evidence of weakness; it is evidence of possibility. Stop measuring your life by where you should have been and start measuring it by where you are willing to go. Your potential is still calling, and it only responds to action.

Don't become so consumed with the success you've had in the past that it stops you from going forward and maximizing your full potential. There's a reason your windshield is larger than your rear-view mirror. The greatest enemy of progress is your last success. Potential demands that you never settle for what you've already accomplished. Yesterday's victories were meant to encourage you - not to imprison you. Success is a milestone, not a monument. If you camp too long on what was, you risk missing what can be. God never reveals your full potential all at once; He unfolds it season by season, step by step. Past success can quietly become a comfort zone. You start reliving old wins instead of pursuing new assignments. But growth demands movement. Faith demands obedience. And potential demands forward motion. The same God who brought you through yesterday's challenges is calling you into greater purpose today. Celebrate where you've been but don't live there.

Your greatest impact is not behind you. It's ahead of you so keep pressing forward, keep stretching, keep trusting, and keep becoming everything God created you to be. Potential is never satisfied with yesterday's victories or paralyzed by today's limitations. It's true, God-given potential is always looks forward. It wakes up each morning with a holy curiosity that asks, "God, what's next?" not out of discontent, but out of devotion. When you walk with God, potential becomes a conversation, not a conclusion. Abraham left what was familiar because God had more ahead. Moses stood at the edge of the Red Sea because God wasn't finished. David refused to live in the shadow of past anointing because God still had battles to win and a kingdom to establish. Potential always leans toward obedience, not comfort. Asking "God, what's next?" is an act of faith. It's the prayer of a servant who knows that potential grows when we stop clinging to what *was* and start listening for what is coming.

Forget about yesterday because God isn't there anymore. That doesn't mean yesterday was meaningless. God used it, He redeemed it, and He taught you through it. But He did not stay there because He is a present-tense God. When He revealed Himself to Moses, He did not say "I was" or "I will be." He said, "I AM." He is not yesterday's God, not tomorrow's God. He is the right-now God. Yesterday is finished. Its power is gone unless you keep giving it permission to rule your mind. Some people stay trapped in yesterday's failures, replaying sins God has already forgiven. Others cling to yesterday's successes, living off old victories while missing today's calling. Both are distractions. God does not anoint your past. He anoints your obedience today. Scripture tells us that God's mercies are new every morning (Lam. 3:23). That means yesterday's mercy expired at midnight. You cannot live today on yesterday's grace. You must step forward and receive what God is pouring out now.

Is. 43:18,19, "Do not remember the former things, nor consider the things of old. Behold, I will do a new thing, now it shall spring forth, shall you not know it?" The Message Bible says, "Forget about what's happened; don't keep going over old history. Be alert, be present. I'm about to do something brand new. It's bursting out! Don't you see it?" New things do not happen in old places. Not one time did God ever duplicate a miracle in the Bible. He is always doing a new thing. God did not create you to live an average, ordinary life. He created you to use your potential and do something new and extraordinary with the purpose you've been given. God is still creating new things, and you have to use your potential to draw out and manifest those things in your life. God is calling you out from the old and into the new. He's calling you to rise to new heights with Him. There is always a newer and bigger mountain to climb. God wants you and Him to climb that mountain together, and the next one after that.

Let yesterday stay where it belongs - behind you. God has already moved on. If you want to walk with Him, you must move on too. Today is where God speaks. Today is where God leads. Today is where God empowers. When you leave the past behind and step into today, you'll discover that God is able to do more than He has already done, and so can you. Jesus said in John 14:12, "Greater things you will do because I go to the Father." Is. 14:24 (MSG) says, "Exactly as I planned, it will happen. Following My blueprints, it will take shape." God had a plan and a blueprint for your life. God is saying to you, "Let's you and Me do something great together." This is not a call based on your strength, your résumé, or your past successes. It is a call rooted in His presence. Think about it: every great work of God began with a person who simply said "yes." Moses had a staff, David had a sling, the disciples had empty nets - but when God joined them, the ordinary became extraordinary.

In the Bible, the first place God introduced potential is found in Gen. 1:11 when He said, "Let the earth bring forth grass, and herb that yields seed, and the fruit tree that yields fruit according to its kind, whose seed is in itself, on the earth." At first glance, it sounds like a simple description of how plants reproduce. But beneath the surface, it reveals the spiritual law of potential that applies not only to creation, but to every life God forms. When God said the seed was in itself, He was declaring that everything He creates carries within it the capacity to become what He intended it to be. A seed does not look like a tree, yet the tree is already there. The fruit is unseen yet already encoded. The harvest is invisible yet already promised. Nothing God makes is dependent on chance to find its purpose. A tree has inside itself the potential to become a forest and an apple has the potential to become an orchard. Likewise, inside of you is the potential to become and do all that God has called you to do.

Potential always precedes performance. God did not wait to see what the seed would become. He defined it before it ever touched the ground. The soil did not decide its identity; the rain did not give it purpose. Those things only assisted growth. The design was already settled. In the same way, your environment does not determine who you are. Your past does not cancel your future. Your current stage does not reveal your full capacity. What you are becoming was placed inside you by God long before circumstances tried to shape you. You may feel small, overlooked, or unfinished but seeds always do. Seeds must be planted, and planting often feels like burial. Darkness, pressure, and waiting are part of the process. The pressure of life cracks the shell so the life inside can emerge. Many seasons that feel like delay are actually seasons of development. God uses hidden places to awaken what is within you. He is not trying to create something new - He is drawing out what He already placed there.

Just like those seeds, you were created with your purpose built into you. God does not create lives and then search for a use for them. Purpose is not discovered by accident; it is revealed through obedience and growth. Just as the seed produces after its kind, you are called to become who God designed you to be - not a copy of someone else, not a reaction to your past, but a fulfillment of your design. Your gifts, calling, and destiny are internal realities waiting to mature. Because potential is hidden, it must be guarded and protected. Fear, comparison, doubt, and distraction all threaten the seed before it ever breaks the surface. The enemy is not intimidated by what you appear to be now but by what you are capable of becoming. Like the seed spoken of at creation, your future is already within you. God has placed purpose inside your life, and in the right season, with faith and obedience, it will emerge. The seed is in itself and so is the potential God placed in you.

One of the greatest gifts God ever gave man is vision, the ability to see beyond the present moment and perceive the end from the beginning. You need to look into the future and see the work God has already finished for this is what propels you forward. Sight is the function of the eyes, but vision is the function of the heart. Sight shows you what is, vision shows you what can be. Sight observes life's circumstances; vision discerns destiny. From the opening pages of Scripture, God reveals Himself as a God who sees the end before the beginning ever unfolds. Vision is the bridge between heaven's intention and earth's reality. This is why the Bible says in 2 Cor. 5:7, "For we walk by faith and not by sight." Vision allows you to see what's already finished. Abraham saw himself as the father of many nations when he was still childless. Joseph saw himself sitting on a throne when he was sitting in a cold prison cell. For the joy that was set before Him, Jesus endured the cross (Heb. 12:2).

Vision is how God speaks to the inner man. Before He ever performs a work in the natural, He paints a picture in the spirit. Noah saw an ark before rain ever fell. Abraham saw descendants before Isaac was born. Joseph saw a throne while still wearing chains. God always shows before He does. That is why scripture declares, "Where there is no vision, the people perish" (Prov.29:18). Without vision, people do not merely struggle - they slowly decay on the inside. Life becomes reactive instead of purposeful. Days turn into survival instead of destiny. Vision gives meaning to suffering and direction to obedience. Vision enables a man to live in the future while standing in the present. It empowers him to endure what others quit because he knows what is coming. When vision is clear, hardship does not confuse - it refines. Delay does not discourage - it develops. A man without vision asks, "Why is this happening to me?" A man with vision asks, "What is this preparing me for?"

Vision is heaven's preview of tomorrow placed inside the human heart today. It is God inviting man to live intentionally, walk faithfully, and finish purposefully. God's vision is rarely comfortable because it demands trust. Vision stretches a man beyond his current capacity. It forces growth. It calls him to walk by faith and not by sight. The very nature of vision means you must believe before you see. This is why many people settle for routine instead of destiny. Vision disrupts comfort. It demands courage. It asks for obedience before explanation. Yet those who embrace vision discover that obedience today unlocks fulfillment tomorrow. Vision distinguishes leaders from followers, builders from spectators, and finishers from quitters. Vision gives a man an internal compass. While others look around for approval, the man with vision looks ahead for direction. He does not measure success by applause but by alignment with God's purpose. It's his duty to finish strong leaving a legacy worth defending.

You are who God says you are and you can do what He says you can do. Your destiny is already determined and each day you're marching toward its fulfillment. Dream big and never focus on your retirement because the word "retirement" is not in the Bible. The sky is the limit for inside of every seed is a forest waiting to spring forth and cover the earth. See yourself doing the things God said you could do and going to the places He said you could go. You are only as big as your dream so believe what God told you. Don't look at what you're going through, look at where you're going to. You've seen the end of your journey, so you know what's happening today is only temporary. Never lose sight of where you're going because dreams are given to give your life direction. You know what to do today because of where you want to be tomorrow. Dreams are like magnets that pull you in the direction of its fulfillment. Grab hold of the dream God gave you and be consumed with having it come to pass.

| 21 |

"EMBRACE YOUR DREAM"

Hab. 2:3 says, "For the vision is yet for an appointed time; But at the end it will speak, and it will not lie. Though it tarries, wait for it; Because it will surely come." The name "Habakkuk" comes from a Hebrew word that means 'embrace.' His name means "one who embraces or clings." Like Habakkuk, God wants you to man up and embrace your dream. The dream stirring in your heart is not an accident, nor is it wishful thinking. It is a divine seed, placed there by God Himself. Too often, people shrink their dreams because of fear, failure, or the opinions of others. The enemy will try to convince you that your dream is unrealistic, too late, or too big. But Scripture reminds us that with God, all things are possible. What seems impossible in your own strength becomes achievable when you walk in obedience and trust. Embracing your dream requires courage. It means stepping out even when the path is unclear. It means believing God when circumstances say otherwise.

242 - RANDALL J. BREWER

Faith is not waiting until everything makes sense - it is moving forward because God said so. God does not reveal dreams to tease you; He reveals them to prepare you. Every delay is not a denial. Every season of waiting is a season of growth. God is shaping your character to match your calling. Do not bury your dream out of fear. Do not abandon it because of past disappointments. Rise up and embrace what God has placed within you. Tend to it with prayer. Protect it with wisdom. Pursue it with diligence. Your dream is bigger than you because it was never meant to be accomplished alone. It was meant to be fulfilled through dependence on God. If God put the dream in your heart, He intends to bring it to pass. Trust Him. Step forward. Man up and embrace the dream He designed for you. Not only does God want you to cling to the call on your life but He also expects you to finish what you begin. Luke 9:62 says. "No one who puts his hand to the plow and looks back is fit for the kingdom of God."

When God places a dream in your heart, He does not do it casually. A God-given dream is a calling, an assignment, and a responsibility. It is not something you visit occasionally - it is something you commit to fully. Jesus' words in Luke 9:62 are sharp, but they are loving. He was not discouraging ambition; He was defining focus. In farming, a man who looks backward while plowing creates crooked rows. The harvest suffers not because the ground was bad, but because the vision was divided. Your God-given dream is the plow in your hands. The moment you say "yes" to God's purpose, you step into the field of destiny. But destiny demands direction. You cannot move forward while constantly glancing over your shoulder at what you left behind longing for what was familiar instead of trusting what God promised. The Bible says to "remember Lot's wife" (Luke 17:32) for a reason. She looked back and was turned into a pillar of salt. She longed for the past and not the future.

When God delivered Lot and his family from the destruction of Sodom, it was an act of mercy. They were told to flee, to not look back, and not to linger. The command was clear, yet Lot's wife looked back. Her body was moving forward, but her heart was still behind. She didn't look back out of curiosity alone. She looked back because something still owned her heart. Sodom had shaped her comfort, her identity, her attachments, and perhaps even her affections. The look back revealed a divided heart. You can leave a place physically and still belong to it emotionally. You can obey God outwardly while resisting Him inwardly. You can walk away with your feet while clinging to the past with your heart. Jesus warned us because looking back freezes spiritual progress, because the dream is before you, not behind. Many dreams die not because God withdrew them, but because the dreamer kept looking back for reassurance instead of forward in faith. Vision demands forward motion, not backward glances.

Dreams require undivided commitment because God does not fulfill dreams in half-hearted people. The Kingdom of God is not built by those who live in the past but by those who look to the future and pursue their dream relentlessly. Fulfillment comes when your hands stay steady on the plow and your eyes remain fixed on the horizon God has set before you. You cannot build tomorrow while clinging to yesterday and this is why Jesus taught us that divided vision disqualifies you for effective service. Faith always looks ahead. God-given dreams are fulfilled by men who man up and refuse to be pulled backward by regret, fear, or the approval of others. The past may explain you, but it does not define you. The future God designed for you requires forward motion. Putting your hand to the plow means you have already started. God is not asking for perfection - He is asking for perseverance. Keep plowing. Keep praying. Keep believing. Stay focused. Straight rows produce strong harvests.

Embrace your dream and keep pressing forward. Cling to the call, run your race, never give up. In other words, man up because God didn't call and anoint you with His power just so you could run away and quit when the going gets tough. God never anoints a man so he can retreat at the first sign of resistance. Heaven does not pour oil on a life just so that life can back away when pressure arrives. When God calls you, He calls you with intention. When He anoints you, He does so with purpose. And when He sends you, He expects you to man up and not shrink back in fear and doubt. The calling of God is not a comfort zone - it is a battleground. Calling invites conflict. Anointing attracts resistance. Purpose provokes opposition. Too many believers confuse God's blessing with ease, but scripture reveals something very different. God's favor often places a man directly in the path of challenge, resistance, and responsibility. The anointing is not given to help you escape the fight; it is given to help you win it.

One of the greatest misconceptions in the Christian walk is the belief that hardship means disobedience. In reality, hardship is often the confirmation that you are walking in divine alignment. If the enemy is opposing you, it is not because you are weak - it is because what God placed inside you is dangerous to the kingdom of darkness. God's anointing is divine empowerment that enables a man to remain faithful under pressure. The oil does not remove the weight; it strengthens the shoulders carrying it. You were anointed so that when things get uncomfortable, you don't quit. You were empowered so that when others walk away, you remain. You were chosen so that when fear whispers retreat, you choose obedience. Running away from difficulty does not bring relief - it brings delay. Sooner or later the same problem will return, and you'll have to face it all over again. Every time a man withdraws in fear and quits a God-given assignment, he trades temporary comfort for long-term frustration.

God does not bless abandonment. He blesses endurance. Quitting always looks easier in the moment. It promises peace, relief, and rest but it never delivers what it advertises. What quitting actually brings is regret. It leaves unanswered questions, unfinished assignments, and a lingering awareness that something sacred was left undone. God never called you to be reckless, but He also never called you to be cowardly. Faith requires courage. Obedience demands resolve. And purpose insists on perseverance. You cannot outrun your calling. You can only delay your destiny. Your biggest enemy is discouragement, but this can be defeated if you refuse to quit. Thomas Edison failed in thousands of experiments and Abraham Lincoln lost several elections. Neither one of these men quit and they both changed the world they lived in. A winner never quits, and quitters never win. Those who refuse to quit eventually overcome, and those who quit never discover what victory requires.

A champion will always look to the future and focus on the outcome of whatever he's trying to do. A champion understands that vision determines direction. If he only looks at the struggle, he will be consumed by it. But when he looks beyond the struggle and toward the outcome - his strength is renewed. Faith is future focused. It calls things that are not as though they already are (Rom. 4:17). The champion walks by faith, not by sight, trusting that God is already working in what cannot yet be seen. Champions who man up don't deny present difficulties; they simply refuse to let present difficulties define their destiny. They know that every trial is shaping endurance, character, and hope. Instead of quitting in the middle of the process, they press forward leaning into it, confident that God finishes what He starts (Phil. 1:6). A champion also understands the power of expectation. What he expects, he moves toward. His heart is set on the finish line, where obedience is rewarded and faith is proven.

Spiritually, a champion lives with eternal perspective. He knows this race is bigger than comfort, applause, or immediate results. He presses forward because he knows who called him and why. Like a runner straining toward the tape, he gives everything he has, not because the path is easy, but because the outcome is worth it. A champion wins long before the victory is visible, when he chooses faith over fear, vision over distraction, and perseverance over retreat. His eyes are forward. His heart is steadfast. And his confidence rests in God who is faithful to bring to pass what He has promised to those who keep moving forward. The children of Israel saw giants in the Promised Land but Caleb saw his mountain. He embraced his dream and hung on to it as he wandered in the wilderness for forty years. Discouragement only comes when you begin to think your dream won't become a reality. Caleb never got discouraged. He kept dreaming. He clung to the call and in the end, he got his mountain.

Dreams are not random thoughts drifting through the mind. They are the imagination of faith reaching forward, touching what God has already prepared, and pulling it into the present. A dream is born when the heart believes, and the mind dares to imagine God's purpose becoming real. God never designed faith to be passive. Faith sees before it touches. Faith imagines before it builds. Long before a promise manifests in the natural, it must first be seen on the inside. The heart becomes the canvas, and the mind becomes the brush. When both are yielded to God, imagination becomes a holy workshop where destiny is formed. God is inviting you to call those things which do not exist as though they did - to see yourself walking in obedience, fruitfulness, and victory long before circumstances agree. When you imagine God's purpose for your life, you are not daydreaming - you are partnering with heaven. Dreams ignite when faith gives imagination permission to rise above limitation.

Faith paints a picture shaped by God's promises rather than human conditions. What you repeatedly see in your heart will eventually seek expression in your life. The enemy works tirelessly to corrupt imagination with fear, doubt, and small thinking. God, however, uses imagination to expand vision, strengthen hope, and anchor faith. What the heart believes and the mind rehearses begins to take root in the soul. Over time, that inner picture demands action, obedience, and perseverance. Dreams become reality when faith refuses to let go of what God has shown you. When you pray, imagine answers. When you plan, imagine fruit. When you walk forward, imagine God's hand guiding every step. Faith-filled imagination gives courage to endure delay and strength to overcome resistance. Your dream is not selfish when it aligns with God's purpose. It is a preview of what obedience will produce. God places dreams within you not to frustrate you, but to draw you forward until the invisible becomes visible.

Let faith shape what you see on the inside because when you do that dreams stop being wishes and begin becoming reality. The truth be told, when you stop dreaming you no longer have a reason to live. Prov. 29:18 says, "Where there is no vision, the people perish." Without dreams there is no desire and without desire there is no hope. Without hope there is no faith and without faith it is impossible to please God. Let's face it, there is something sacred about a dream. A dream is more than an idea - it is a whisper from God reminding you that your life still has purpose. When a person stops dreaming, it's not because God has stopped working. It's usually because disappointment, delay, or pain has tried to convince them that hoping is too costly. But heaven never asks you to stop dreaming but God to trust while you wait. He placed dreams inside you long before you ever faced your first obstacle. Those dreams were not accidents. They were seeds planted by a Creator who sees the end from the beginning.

The dream is proof that your story is not finished. The enemy doesn't fight you because of your past - he fights you because of your future. If he can silence your dream, he can weaken your desire. And when desire fades, so does expectancy. But expectancy is the atmosphere where miracles are born. Scripture tells us that God is able to do "exceedingly abundantly above all that we ask or think" (Eph. 3:20). Notice the words "ask or think." As long as you can still imagine, believe, and dream, God has something to work with. Dreaming keeps your spirit alive. It gives you something to rise up for in the morning and something to reach toward when the road feels long. You may feel tired. You may feel delayed. You may feel wounded. But weariness does not disqualify you - only surrendering your dream does. And God never asked you to bury what He told you to carry. And as long as there is breath in your body, there is still a reason to believe, a reason to rise, and a reason to live.

It is in your dreams and faith imaginations that you meet God and experience His divine power. Your dream is where you come face-to-face with the living God. It's your meeting place with the King of kings and Lord of lords. When you dream you are saying, "Lord, I put my hope and trust in You." This is faith, the place where God meets with His people. God has always revealed Himself in this way. Abraham saw a future filled with descendants before he ever held a son. Joseph dreamed of leadership while still wearing the chains of slavery. Jacob dreamed of a ladder reaching into heaven and awoke knowing God was nearby. Before the miracle arrived, the vision came first. Faith imaginations are not fantasy; it is the womb of divine possibility. It is where God paints pictures of His will upon the canvas of your spirit. When the Holy Spirit stirs your imagination, He is inviting you to man up and come up higher, to see what God sees, to believe with all your heart everything He has promised.

Many people limit God because they limit their ability to see beyond the present moment. But faith dares to see what is not yet visible. Faith imagines healing before the symptoms leave. Faith imagines restoration while broken pieces still lie on the floor. Faith imagines victory while the battle still rages. This is not denial of reality - it is alignment with divine truth. Dreams from God ignite hope, strengthen endurance, and anchor the soul in difficult seasons. They remind us that our lives are part of a greater story authored by a faithful God. When you guard your dreams, meditate on God's promises, and allow the Spirit to expand your vision, you position yourself to experience God's power in real and tangible ways. Do not despise the holy dreams God places in your heart. Do not silence the faith-filled images He gives you in prayer. Those moments when your spirit sees beyond what your eyes can see are often where God reveals His direction, releases His peace, and prepares you for His next move.

What God reveals to you in the spirit, He is faithful to bring to pass in your life. He is a miracle-working God and He lives in the realm of the impossible. This is where you should live also. God gives you big dreams and calls you to do the impossible because He wants to be involved in everything you do. If what you are called to do is possible with natural gifts and abilities, then God would not be needed. He gives impossible dreams so you'll seek Him out for divine help, guidance, and intervention. When a vision is bigger than your strength, wisdom, or resources, it forces you to lift your eyes beyond yourself. Impossible dreams expose your limitations so you will seek His divine help, depend on His guidance, and trust His intervention. What you cannot accomplish on your own becomes the very place where God reveals His power. When the dream is too heavy to carry alone, it will lead you to your knees and it is there you discover that with God, the impossible becomes a testimony of His glory and grace.

Prov. 16:9 says, "A man's heart plans his way, but the Lord directs his steps." This verse is saying that you and God are partners together in the fulfillment of your divine purpose. Don't forget that God demands your involvement in everything He calls you to do. More times than not, God will not do His part until you first do your part so start making plans for the things you can do and actions you can take. It's when you step out of the boat that God steps in and directs your steps. Remember, a parked car goes nowhere. Dreams are given to be fulfilled so always aim high. Always expect the best. Man up and go for the top. A mountain climber always sets his sights on the top of the mountain that is before him. The proof of desire is pursuit so don't sit around and wait for your dream's fulfillment to come to you. Set goals for whatever needs to be done. Make plans and apply works to your faith. Pursue your dream. Man up and take action! With confident expectancy look for your dream to become a reality.

| 22 |

"ENLARGE YOUR VISION"

There is a destiny inside of you waiting to be released. God did not create you to drift, coast, or merely survive. He created you to carry weight, to stand firm, and to fulfill an assignment. Inside of you is a God-given destiny placed there before the world ever tried to define you, limit you, or break you. Long before you faced pressure, responsibility, or disappointment, God deposited purpose in you. He wired you with strength, leadership, courage, and resolve. That destiny may be covered right now - buried under failure, fear, exhaustion, or compromise - but it is not dead. It is waiting to be released. Many men feel restless but can't explain why. They succeed outwardly yet feel unsettled inwardly. That uneasiness is not weakness - it is the spirit of God reminding you that you were made for more than comfort, more than routine, more than playing it safe. Destiny does not respond to passivity. It responds to obedience. God releases destiny when a man decides to stand up, take responsibility, and move forward.

You don't need to feel ready; you need to be willing. Every step of faith unlocks what God already placed inside you. Understand that destiny is not released in ease - it is forged in pressure. God builds men in hidden places before He uses them in public ones. Delays are not denials. Struggle is not failure. The seasons where no one sees you are often the seasons where God is making you strong enough to carry what's coming. Stop judging your future by your past. Your mistakes did not disqualify you. Your wounds did not cancel your calling. God specializes in restoring men who thought they were finished. The world does not need more passive men - it needs men of conviction. Men who pray when it's hard. Men who lead when it's uncomfortable. Men who stand when others bow. Your destiny is connected to others - your family, your church, your community - and when you fail to rise, others suffer the loss. But when a man steps into his God-given destiny, everything changes.

You've been called to do more with your life than you've already done. As long as there is breath inside of you, there will always be more for you to do for you have not reached the end of your calling. What you have done so far - your victories, your failures, your lessons, your scars - were not the destination. They were preparation. God never sustains life without purpose. Every heartbeat is a reminder that your assignment is still active. If your work were complete, your time would be complete. But you are still here - still standing, still breathing, still able to choose, still able to serve, still able to grow. That means there is more for you to do. More faith to exercise. More love to give. More truth to speak. More ground to take. More people to influence. More obedience to walk in. The enemy would like you to believe your best days are behind you - that you've already done enough, suffered enough, given enough. But God says otherwise. He does not call men to coast; He calls them to finish strong.

There is more inside of you than you have released. More strength than you have tested. More courage than you have required of yourself. God placed greatness within you not for applause, but for impact. The clock of heaven has not run out on your life. The mission is not over. The call has not been withdrawn. As long as there is breath in your lungs, there will always be more for you to do—and God will supply everything you need to do it. Jabez prayed, "Oh, that you would bless me and enlarge my territory" (1 Chron. 4:10). You must get rid of small thinking and having a limited view of what you're capable of doing. Understand that wanting to do more for God causes you to believe for more opportunities for ministry to happen. God designed desire to be a doorway - not a distraction. Wanting more is not greed when it is rooted in faith; it is often the first signal that God is stirring something deeper within your spirit. Desire awakens belief. Before a man ever reaches higher, he must first want to go higher.

Wanting more stretches the heart beyond comfort. It challenges the lie that says, "This is as good as it gets." Holy desire refuses to settle for less than what is available. Instead, let it drive you closer to God and to stretch your faith. Belief is born where desire meets trust. When you want more of God, you begin to expect more from God. Faith does not grow in apathy;

it grows in hunger. Scripture says God rewards those who diligently seek Him, not those who casually acknowledge Him. Wanting more drives you to seek, knock, ask, and stand when others quit. Desire fuels vision. You cannot believe for what you do not want. Wanting more causes you to lift your eyes beyond your current limitations and see what God sees. It moves you from survival thinking to promise thinking. The man who wants more starts praying differently, speaking differently, and walking differently because his expectations have changed. Do not silence holy hunger. Let it pull you into the "more" God has already prepared for you.

Is. 54:2 says, "Enlarge the place of your tent, and let them stretch out the curtains of your habitations; Do not spare; Lengthen your cords, and strengthen your stakes." To enlarge the place of your tent means to enlarge your vision. Many people limit God by the size of their expectation. They believe only for what they can see, afford, or control. But God says, "Make it bigger." Increase your faith. Expand your thinking. Refuse to let past disappointments determine future possibilities. To stretch out the curtains is to remove restrictions. Curtains define boundaries. God is saying, "Push the limits." Stop confining your faith to what feels safe or familiar. Stretch beyond comfort. Stretch beyond fear. Stretch beyond what you have known, because God is about to do something greater than what you have experienced. What He is about to do will reveal His greater purpose, deeper power, and overwhelming grace. Stay expectant; the next move of God will be bigger than anything you've known.

The phrase "Do not spare" is a command to act boldly. Half-hearted faith produces half-hearted results. God is calling for full obedience, full trust, and full surrender. This is not the season to hold back, shrink back, or play it safe. This is the season to believe big and move decisively. To lengthen your cords speaks of increasing your reach. Cords connect the tent to the stakes. God is telling you to extend your influence, your faith, your prayers, and your obedience. Reach further than you ever have before. Believe for more impact, more fruit, and more effectiveness in the Kingdom. Finally, to strengthen your stakes is to deepen your foundation. Expansion without stability leads to collapse. As God enlarges your life, your calling, and your influence, He also requires stronger roots. Strengthen your commitment to the Word. Strengthen your prayer life. Strengthen your character. What God is preparing to build through your life must be firmly grounded in truth and unwavering faithfulness.

Isaiah 54:2 is a prophetic invitation to prepare for increase. God is saying, "I am ready to do more. Are you ready to receive more." If so, then enlarge your vision, stretch your faith, and act without fear. Strengthen your foundation because when God commands you to make room, it is only because He intends to fill it. Just be made aware that your limitations determine the size of your tent. To enlarge your tent, you've got to think bigger than you've ever thought before. God is saying that your tent is not to stay the same size. Expand your thinking about what God wants to do in your life. Enlarge your capacity to receive what God wants to do in you and through you. Go beyond thinking about getting your own needs met and allow God to use you to meet the needs of others. God wants to bless you so you can be a blessing to those around you. Man up and enlarge your vision and prepare to receive more and prepare to give more. Make your life count. After all, that's what being a man of God is all about.

David said in Ps. 23:5, "My cup runs over." This means he had more than enough. When Jesus fed the multitude there were twelve baskets left over. They also had more than enough. Don't pray to just get by, pray that you'll have more than enough so you'll be able to help others in need. A warrior does not train to barely survive the battle. He trains to win, to protect, and to provide yet many men pray like refugees instead of warriors. They pray, "Lord, just help me hang on." Those prayers may keep you alive, but they will never position you for victory. God did not create men to live on the edge of defeat. He created men to stand in the gap, to carry weight, and to be strong enough to help others when pressure hits. A warrior doesn't pray survival prayers so he can get by barely making it through the day. No, he prays to have more than enough because he knows God never called His people to live on the edge of lack. He called us to live as channels, not containers, in order to pass the blessing on to others.

God's heart has always been abundance with purpose. When you pray only to get by, your vision stays small. But when you pray for more than enough, your life becomes a blessing in motion. God doesn't bless you so you can hoard, He blesses you so you can help, heal, lift, and restore. Be willing to ask big, for more than what you need. Ask for those abundant blessings that will propel you to your destiny and purpose. God wants you to "be complete, thoroughly equipped for every good work" (2 Tim. 3:17). No longer are you to have a survival mentality. Man up and ask big and receive big. Enlarge your vision and stop having your problems on your mind all the time. Survival is the enemy of your God-given dream because survival weakens the warrior's vision. A man trapped in survival mode becomes inward-focused. His world shrinks to bills, stress, fear, and exhaustion. When a man is only trying to survive, he has no margin to lead, no strength to serve, and no resources to rescue.

God never sent warriors into battle hoping they had just enough strength. He trained them, armed them, and surrounded them so they could prevail. If your prayers only ask for survival, your life will never rise above maintenance. Warriors are not called to maintain ground - they are called to take ground. This is why God supplies warriors for the sake of others. God's blessings are not rewards for comfort; they are tools for responsibility. A warrior with more than enough feeds those who cannot feed themselves, protects those who cannot defend themselves, and carries burdens others would collapse under. God looks for men who can be trusted with weight. Increase is not about luxury - it is about load-bearing strength. If God can trust you to lift others when they fall, He will strengthen your arms. You'll go from self-preservation to kingdom provision. Men are called to be providers, not just for their homes, but for their communities. Not just financially, but spiritually, emotionally, and relationally.

From the very beginning, God's nature has been one of abundance. Creation itself was excessive. There was more beauty, more provision, more potential than Adam and Eve could ever consume alone. Scarcity entered the world through sin, not through God's design. Throughout Scripture, whenever God stepped into a situation, He did not bring just enough - He brought overflow. Manna fell daily, teaching trust, not desperation. Water flowed from a rock in the wilderness and oil multiplied in a widow's jar until there were no more containers. Bread and fish multiplied until thousands were fed and an abundance of leftovers remained. These were not accidents. They were revelations of God's heart. God supplies more than enough because He thinks beyond the individual. He always sees the crowd, the community, and the future. This is why His warriors don't just pray for excess - they pray for effectiveness. When you man up and ask God for more than enough, you are asking for a larger assignment.

Warriors pray for overflow, not comfort. Comfort makes men passive. Overflow makes men purposeful. A kingdom warrior measures success by impact, not accumulation. His life is not defined by what he owns, but by who he lifts up. When God gives a warrior more than enough his home becomes a refuge, his hands become provision, and his life becomes a testimony. He becomes the man others call when things fall apart. Men were not created to barely make it. They were created to build, protect, and provide. Don't pray to just get by, pray to be strong enough to help others stand. That is the prayer of a warrior. Understand that a big God needs to be asked for big things. God created the entire universe so why would you go to Him asking for little things? God is not intimidated by the impossible. With Him, there is no such thing. He is not offended when you ask Him for big things, He's disappointed when you ask Him for anything less. Prayers that are not impossible to you are insulting to God.

God is ready to act if you're bold enough to ask. Know with certainty that He will move heaven and earth on your behalf. If He can part the Red Sea, He can answer your prayers for big things. Come boldly to God with your big request knowing that prayer changes things. Jer. 33:3 says, "Call to Me, and I will answer you, and show you great and mighty things." Man up and don't ask God for only five loaves and two fish. No, ask Him for the twelve baskets that were left over. Don't be shy and don't hold back. Ask big and receive big. Don't ask for finances to pay your monthly mortgage payment, ask for the entire loan to be paid off. Then ask Him to help you pay somebody else's mortgage off. Come up higher and ask God for what you really want. He is honored that you believe He's big enough to give it to you. God said in Ps. 2:8, "Only ask, and I will give you the nations as your inheritance, the whole earth as your possessions." What could be bigger than that? Pray boldly and expect abundantly.

God gives more than enough so that the hungry can be fed, the weary can be strengthened, the broken can be restored, and the lost can be reached. When God knows that blessing you will result in blessing others, He'll release more into your hands. Heaven responds to hearts that say, "Lord, if You give it to me, I will use it for Your glory." Enlarge your vision and go find people to bless. Gal. 5:13 (MSG) says, "God has called you to a free life. Use your freedom to serve one another in love." God wants to use you as a channel through which His blessings flow into the lives of other people. He didn't heal your back so you could play more golf. He healed you so you would be physically ready to help others in need. He doesn't bless you financially just so you can pay your bills but so you'll be able to pay someone else's bills also. Daily look for opportunities to be a blessing to somebody. Seek and you will find. Life only has meaning when you are used by God to help make somebody else's life better.

There is a better life to live than what the world offers. There are not enough pleasures in this world to give your life purpose, meaning, and satisfaction. 1 Cor. 15:19 (NLT) says, "And if our hope in Christ is only for this life, we are more to be pitied than anyone in the world." Come up to a higher way of living and step into the plan God has for your life. The more you grow in Christ and get used by Him, the less you'll desire the lustful pleasures of this world. This is not because temptation vanishes, but because something greater has taken its place. The more you grow in Christ, the more your appetite changes. When a person is shallow in their walk with God, the world still looks attractive. Its pleasures glitter. Its lusts promise satisfaction. Its shortcuts seem reasonable. When you enlarge your vision and as you draw closer to Christ - walking with Him daily, submitting to His Word, and allowing Him to use you - those same things begin to feel empty, noisy, and beneath the calling placed on your life.

A nationwide survey was taken where people were asked if they could ask God one question, what would it be? The answer most people gave was, "Why am I here?" The majority of people in the world today don't know why they're here. Instead of finding out they have the attitude that "whatever will be, will be." They take whatever life throws at them instead of taking charge of their destiny and finding out what God wants them to do. These are the people who die with nothing to show for their lives. They lived their life in vain, a life with no meaning and purpose. Not long after they're dead and gone the world will forget they were even here. Don't be like these people. A small vision produces a small life. But a God-given vision stretches a man beyond comfort, beyond convenience, and beyond self-preservation. God never enlarges a man's vision just so he can live better - He enlarges it so. Man up and enlarge your vision so you can help make the lives of other people better and your legacy will last forever.

When a man refuses to think small, he refuses to live selfishly. He understands that his strength isn't just for survival - it's for service. His success isn't just for enjoyment - it's for impact. His life isn't just about getting to heaven - it's about bringing heaven into the lives of others. Legacy is not what you accumulate; it is what you activate in others. It's the lives you strengthen, the faith you ignite, the courage you model, and the hope you pass on. Long after your name is no longer spoken, your influence continues to speak through the people you invested in. To man up is to stop living with a short horizon. It's to realize that God has entrusted you with strength, wisdom, resources, and influence - not to hoard them, but to multiply them. The man who dares to enlarge his vision becomes a builder of people, a defender of purpose, and a carrier of God's heart. When your vision grows, your impact grows. When your impact grows, lives are changed. And when lives are changed, your legacy echoes into eternity.

| 23 |

"A HOLY CALLING"

There are two narrow roads mentioned in the Bible. Matt. 7:13 says, "Enter by the narrow gate." This is the narrow road to eternal life. Matt. 20:16 says, "For many are called, but few are chosen." This is the narrow road of the chosen few. The call to service in God's kingdom goes out to everyone. God calls all men to salvation. He calls all men to purpose. He calls all men to obedience, holiness, and surrender. The invitation is broad. The door is open. Grace is extended freely. But the chosen are not merely those who hear the call. They are the ones who man up and respond to it with courage and determination. Many hear God's voice, but few rearrange their lives around it. Many admire Jesus, but few follow Him when the road becomes narrow. Many want the crown, but few are willing to carry the cross. Both these roads are narrow and difficult and, yes, there are few who find them. It is estimated that 10% of Christians do 90% of the work. God is asking you today, "Which road will you travel on?"

The chosen few are those who allow God to shape them, correct them, refine them, and stretch them. They don't just want God's blessings - they want God's will. They don't just want heaven later - they want heaven on earth now. God does not choose men based on talent, strength, or popularity. He chooses them based on their obedience, faithfulness, and submission. The tragedy is not that few are chosen; the tragedy is that many never move beyond the call. Today, the question is not, "Am I called?" The question is, "Am I willing to respond to the call?" The call on your life is not random, accidental, or self-generated. It is holy - set apart by God, conceived in heaven, and released on earth with divine intention. Before you ever recognized it, God had already spoken it. Before you ever stepped into it, heaven had already endorsed it. 2 Tim. 1:9 says God "has saved us and called us with a holy calling." A holy call means your purpose did not originate in human ambition but in divine design.

Man up and take your call very seriously. It wasn't something you came up with on your own but was decided by God Himself. You don't decide your calling, you discover it. God sees your potential and what you're capable of doing. He doesn't see who you are today, He sees what you can become. Because the call is holy, the purpose is sacred. It is not merely about success, recognition, or achievement - it is about advancing God's will on the earth. Your calling is meant to reflect His nature, reveal His heart, and release His power through your life. A holy calling always carries responsibility because it represents God. It carries weight because eternity is involved. It carries impact because lives are affected. What God has placed on your life is not common; therefore, you cannot live carelessly and still fulfill it. A holy call demands that your life belongs to God for His purposes. Certain paths, habits, and compromises may no longer fit because your calling requires clarity, integrity, and obedience.

A holy calling is when God says, "I have marked you for My use." God never issues a holy calling without providing holy power. The same God who calls also equips, strengthens, and sustains. When the assignment feels bigger than you, that is confirmation that God intends to be involved. You are not expected to fulfill your calling by human effort alone. You are empowered by the Holy Spirit, God's wisdom, God's timing, and God's strength. Because your call is divine in nature, it is divine in purpose. Heaven stands behind it. Angels are assigned to it. Doors open at the right time. Resistance may come, but opposition is often evidence that your call carries weight. The enemy does not fight what does not matter. Your calling is not just about where you are going but is about who God intends to reach through you. Do not treat lightly what God has declared holy. Do not shrink it to fit comfort, fear, or convenience. You were not called to blend in - you were called with a holy calling to stand out for God's glory.

A problem with a lot of men today is they don't know how to get their assignment from God. Yes, they genuinely love God, pray regularly, attend church faithfully and yet still live with a quiet frustration in their soul. They ask, "Why do I feel unfulfilled? Why does it feel like I'm busy but not purposeful?" One of the greatest mistakes men make is assuming that good activity equals divine assignment. Just because something is good does not mean it is assigned by God. You can be doing a meaningful work and still be missing the specific work God called you to do. There is a specific assignment God has placed on every life, and fulfillment only comes when we walk in it. Another mistake men make is they think God hands out assignments and they're supposed to adapt to those plans whether they like it or not. No, this is not how heavenly callings are given to committed servants. God's will and your desires work hand-in-hand. What you enjoy doing the most is a clue to what God wants you to do with your life.

God wants you to be happy in your service to Him, not miserable. Many men spend their lives trying to figure out what God wants them to do, while overlooking one of the clearest indicators He has already given them: joy. Whatever brings you the most joy can be used for the Kingdom of God. Eccl. 3:22 says, "Wherefore I perceive that there is nothing better than that a man should rejoice in his own works, for that is his heritage." Eccl. 5:20 says, "God keeps every man busy with the joy of his heart." God is not a taskmaster who assigns burdens without purpose. He is a Father who places holy delight inside His children - desires that point toward destiny. Joy is not random; it is often revelation in seed form. Phil. 2:13 says that God is the One who works in us "both to will and to do His good pleasure." That means the desires that align with righteousness are not accidents - they are God-initiated. Joy is often the language God uses to whisper, "This is where I can use you."

Too many people believe serving God means abandoning everything they love. In reality, God often redeems, redirects, and multiplies what already brings you joy. Religion says, "Stop enjoying life and start serving God." The kingdom says, "Let God take what you enjoy and make it eternal." Jesus was anointed "with the oil of gladness" (Heb. 1:9). The early church served God with glad hearts, not heavy ones. Joy does not compete with holiness - it fuels it. When joy is present passion replaces pressure, faithfulness outlasts fatigue, excellence becomes natural, and perseverance becomes possible. God's work done God's way produces God's joy. God is not looking to use only preachers and missionaries. He is looking to use musicians, builders, thinkers, organizers, encouragers, innovators, leaders, caregivers, creators, and servants all fueled by joy and guided by obedience. Your greatest joy is pointing toward your greatest contribution. When joy and purpose unite, the Kingdom advances.

When you give God what brings you the most joy, He gives your life the deepest meaning. Men are often taught that strength means endurance without enjoyment. But in the Kingdom of God, joy is not weakness; joy is fuel. Whatever brings you the most joy can be used for the Kingdom of God. God did not create men to live drained, directionless, and defeated. He created warriors - men who know why they fight, who they serve, and where they are most effective. A warrior is most dangerous where he is fully alive. Joy is not comfort - it is alignment. It marks the place where your strength, passion, and God's purpose intersect. When a man fights in the wrong arena, he burns out. When he fights where God designed him to fight, he becomes unstoppable. David didn't find joy in Saul's armor. He found it with a sling in his hand. In the same way, when a man refuses to imitate others and instead embraces the role God shaped him for, fear loses its voice, and resistance loses its power.

The Kingdom does not need more bored men or burned-out men. It needs engaged men - men who know their weapon, their assignment, and their King. Your joy is not a distraction; it is part of your design. Give it to God and let Him sharpen it. Then man up and go take your place on the battlefield knowing God doesn't want anybody working for Him who doesn't want to do what they're doing. The truth be told, if you're not having fun, you're in the wrong call. Why? Because there is power in desire. Desire is the spark that awakens the heart. When a man truly wants something - when his desire is clear and focused - it gives birth to excitement. That excitement stirs the soul, and from it flows energy: the drive to move, to act, to pursue. Where desire is alive, energy follows, and what once felt impossible suddenly feels within reach. Desire stirs up your passion and the anointing to fulfill your call. Many are called, but few are chosen because too few have the desire to pursue what the call demands.

Rom. 12:11 says to be "not lagging in diligence, fervent in spirit, serving the Lord." To be "fervent in spirit" means to be aglow and burning with the Spirit of God in your heart. Eccl. 9:10 says, "Whatever your hand finds to do, do it with all your might." Paul said, "I press toward the goal for the prize of the upward call of God in Christ Jesus" (Phil. 3:14). Run after your call the same way David ran toward the giant. When you give your all to God, God will give His all to you (Rom. 8:28). Be motivated by the vision deep in your heart. Helen Keller said the one thing worse than being blind was having no vision. Prov. 29:18 says, "Where there is no vision, the people perish." Those who are successful in life have a God-given vision and are motivated by it. Remember, you've only got one life to live. You can live it any way you want but you can only live it once. The good news is that if you do it right, once is enough. Man up and press on! Go forward and be all that you can be. Make your life count.

Most people view success differently from how God views success. The world says you need houses, cars, boats, real estate, and lots of money to be successful. Joseph had none of these. He was a slave in Egypt, yet the Bible says he was a successful man. He was successful and prosperous because the Lord was with him. True success in life is not measured by titles, wealth, applause, or recognition. Real success is determined by one thing alone: the manifested presence of God wherever you go. Many people chase success, but Scripture teaches us that success follows presence. When God's presence is with a person, favor, wisdom, protection, and increase accompany them naturally. Without His presence, even the most talented individual eventually struggles, but with His presence, ordinary people do extraordinary things. The Bible emphasizes this truth. When God was with Joseph, everything he touched prospered whether he was in Potiphar's house, in prison, or in the palace.

Joseph had a holy calling and even though his circumstances changed, the presence of God did not. And because of that, success followed him into every environment he was in. It was not Joseph's position that brought success; it was God's presence resting upon him. Wherever the presence of God is welcomed, confusion gives way to clarity, fear bows to peace, lack yields to provision, and opposition loses its power. The presence of God turns barren places into fruitful ones and hostile environments into platforms for promotion. This is why Moses boldly declared, "If Your presence does not go with us, do not send us from here" (Ex. 33:15). Moses understood that movement without God's presence is failure, no matter how impressive your holy calling looks. But progress with God's presence guarantees purpose, direction, and victory. Your success will never be sustained by effort alone. It is sustained by alignment with God's will, God's voice, and God's presence.

When you carry His presence, you carry authority. When you walk in His presence, doors open that effort could never force open. When you honor His presence, you become a living testimony that God is real, active, and involved. This is how a holy calling gets fulfilled. The goal of the believer is not to build a life God visits occasionally, but a life where His presence abides continually. When God's presence rests on you, success becomes a byproduct rather than a pursuit. You don't chase success - it follows you. So seek His presence above platforms. Value His presence more than promotion. Protect His presence more than popularity. Because where God's presence is manifested, failure cannot remain, and success becomes inevitable. When the Lord is with you success will come with little or no effort. You'll be able to do things you wouldn't ordinarily be able to do on your own. You'll be a funnel through which the favor of God can flow into the lives of other people. That's what being a man is all about.

Joseph was successful because God was with him. Why was Joseph blessed? So he could be a blessing to Egypt and his family. Start looking around to see who you can be a blessing to. Who needs a word of encouragement? Who is carrying a burden too heavy for them alone? Who feels unseen, overlooked, or forgotten? You're here to make the lives of other people better. Purpose begins when your eyes lift from yourself and start scanning the world around you. There are people within arm's reach of your life right now who need inspiration, help, strength, kindness, or hope and God positioned you there on purpose. It doesn't take much to be a blessing. Sometimes a blessing is as simple as listening. Sometimes it's showing up when others walk away. Sometimes it's giving compassion, time, wisdom, or practical help. In the presence of God are blessings galore and you need to leave a trail of blessings wherever you go. Do something that will cause people to say, "The Lord is in this place."

Allow God to use you to bless someone else because they've been in your presence a little while. A holy calling is not merely about being set apart from the world - it is about being sent into it with God's heart. When God calls a person, He does not only call them upward; He calls them outward. True holiness is never cold, distant, or detached. It is warm with mercy, alive with grace, and active in love. Compassion is the visible evidence of a divine calling. God never separates calling from caring. From the beginning, His purpose has always been relational - restoring what is broken, healing what is wounded, and lifting those who have fallen. A holy calling that lacks compassion becomes religion without reflection of God's character. Jesus demonstrated this perfectly. He was holy beyond measure, yet He touched lepers, wept with the grieving, fed the hungry, and forgave the guilty. His holiness did not isolate Him from people - it drew Him closer to them. Follow His example and do the same.

Those who are truly called by God will feel the weight of others' pain. A holy calling sharpens your sensitivity to suffering rather than numbing it. It moves you beyond judgment into mercy, beyond words into deeds, and beyond comfort into sacrifice. Compassion becomes the bridge between heaven's purpose and earth's need. You must remember that people may never read your calling, but they will always experience your compassion. Love opens hearts where doctrine alone cannot. Kindness softens resistance. Mercy reflects the very nature of God. When compassion flows through your life, your holy calling becomes credible and Christ becomes visible. A holy calling is fulfilled not only in prayer and proclamation, but in showing up, lifting burdens, and loving people where they are. Compassion is the proof that our calling is real, alive, and working through your words and actions. To be called by God is to carry His heart. To carry His heart is to live with love and compassion at all times.

Many people treat blessings like trophies - proof of God's favor meant to be admired and protected. But in the Kingdom of God, blessings are more like seeds. Seeds are useless if stored away; they only fulfill their purpose when planted. God blesses you with resources so you can meet needs. He blesses you with wisdom so you can guide others. He blesses you with healing so you can bring hope. He blesses you with strength so you can lift the weary. What God pours into you is meant to be poured out. You were never meant to be a reservoir - you were meant to be a river. Blessings are designed to flow through you, not stop with you. God could meet every need on earth without human involvement, but He chooses not to. Instead, He partners with His people. He feeds the hungry through willing hands. He comforts the broken through compassionate hearts. He finances kingdom work through obedient stewards. When God blesses you, He is saying, "I know I can move this through you."

The question is not how much has God given you, the real question is, "How much can God trust you to pass it on?" A closed fist cannot receive but an open hand stays ready to give and ready to receive. When you live with open hands, blessings circulate freely, joy multiplies, and God's presence becomes evident in your life. The most fulfilled believers are not those who accumulate the most, but those who release the most. They understand that the true blessing of life is the participation of doing God's work on the earth. You have a holy calling so let the blessings flow. Don't dam up what God designed to move through you. Don't hoard what heaven meant to bless others with. You are blessed so others can be blessed through you. And when you live that way, you'll discover the powerful truth that the more you let God's blessings flow through you, the more He ensures they keep flowing to you. God guarantees that you are never emptied. The more you pour out, the more He pours in.

| 24 |

"THE MAN GOD WANTS"

In every generation, men ask some version of the same question, "What does it mean to be a good man?" Culture answers with shifting standards, with worldly things like success, strength, popularity, wealth, dominance, or comfort. But God's answer has never changed. The question is not merely what kind of man you want to be, but what kind of man does God want you to be. The man God wants is not a myth, nor a relic of the past. He is not defined by bravado, arrogance, or outward show. He is not measured by titles, applause, or social media affirmation. The man God wants is shaped in secret places, refined by obedience, and strengthened through surrender. He is forged through truth, humility, courage, and faith. God is not looking for flawless men - He is looking for men who will show up, men who will stay surrendered, and men who will keep trusting Him even when they fall short. Faithful men get up when they fall, repent when they miss the mark, and obey even when the outcome is uncertain.

God is not waiting for you to become flawless before He uses you. He is waiting for you to be available, obedient, and faithful right where you are. Men often believe the lie that they must conquer every weakness before they can be used by God but that is not how He works. Every man God used in Scripture had scars - internal and external. God didn't wait for them to clean up their mess before calling them into battle. He called them in the middle of it. He's not looking for perfection; He's looking for faithfulness and availability. In battle, the soldier who shows up matters more than the one who looks good on paper. God isn't asking for a perfect résumé - He's asking for a man who will step forward when the call goes out. Men disqualify themselves by saying, "I'm not ready. I've failed too much. I'm still working through things." But the battlefield has never been won by perfect men - only present ones. A warrior says, "I may not be perfect but I'm reporting for duty anyway. Here I am, Lord. Send me."

Wars are won by men who hold their ground day after day. Faithfulness is staying engaged when the excitement fades and the fight becomes exhausting. Faithful men keep praying when nothing seems to change, keep serving when no one notices, and keep standing when it would be easier to quit. God entrusts authority to men who prove they can be trusted with consistency. You don't need to be impressive, but you do need to be dependable. God does not wait until a man is battle-ready before using him. The fight itself is what forges the warrior. Weakness is a training ground for manhood. God will shape your character, refine your discipline, and build your strength as you obey. Men who wait for perfection never enter the fight. Men who are faithful step forward and are transformed in it. The kingdom of God is not built by spectators, critics, or comfort-seekers. It is built by men who are available, obedient, and faithful, by men who show up imperfect but willing, by men who rise up and report for duty.

One of the first things we learn in scripture is that God seeks "a man after His own heart" (1 Sam. 13:14). That statement sets the tone for how God works with humanity. Before He looks for ability, He looks for alignment. Before He entrusts authority, He searches the inner man. God was not merely looking for a king to occupy a throne - He was seeking a man whose desires, values, and motives reflected His own. This reveals something critical: God's primary concern has never been outward success, but inward surrender. A man after God's own heart is not a flawless man. David would later fail, stumble, and even sin grievously. Yet his life teaches us that God is drawn to repentant hearts, humble spirits, and teachable souls. God is not impressed by perfection; He is moved by devotion. To be "after God's heart" means to pursue what God loves and to grieve over what grieves Him. It means to man up and choose obedience over convenience, truth over comfort, and faith over fear.

God is still seeking for men who will place their hearts fully in His hands. When God finds a heart that beats in rhythm with His own, He can shape it, strengthen it, and use it to impact generations. Authority flows from intimacy, calling flows from character, and legacy flows from a heart fully yielded to God. The man God wants guards his heart carefully. He understands that what he allows into his mind and spirit will eventually shape his character. He does not flirt with sin and then act surprised when it takes root. He does not excuse compromise with phrases like "everyone does it" or "it's not that bad." A man after God's heart loves what God loves, hates what God hates, repents quickly when he falls, and hungers for God's presence more than personal comfort. God is not impressed with outward religion when the heart is far from Him. He desires authenticity - real devotion, real humility, real obedience. He is drawn to hearts that hunger for Him, not hands that merely go through motions.

A real man does not measure his strength by how loud he is, how much he controls, or how many people fear him. A real man measures his life by how deeply he fears the Lord. The fear of the Lord is not terror; it is reverence. It is a deep awareness that God is holy, sovereign, and worthy of obedience. The man God wants does not treat God casually or speak of Him lightly. He does not reduce God to a mascot for personal ambition. A man who fears God understands accountability. He knows that his life is lived before the eyes of heaven. He chooses integrity not because someone is watching, but because God always is. A man who fears the Lord understands that there is a higher authority than his emotions, his ambitions, or his reputation. A man who fears the Lord chooses integrity when no one is watching. He stands firm when compromise would be easier. He disciplines his thoughts, his words, and his actions because he knows he answers to God before he answers to anyone else.

This kind of fear produces courage, not cowardice. It creates backbone, not insecurity. The fear of the Lord teaches a man to hate what is evil and cling to what is good. It restrains him from arrogance and keeps him humble. It gives him clarity in confusion and direction in chaos. When storms come - and they will - a God-fearing man does not panic. He stands steady because his confidence is not in himself, but in the Lord. A real man fears the Lord because he knows that leadership begins with submission. He cannot lead his family, his calling, or his generation unless he is first led by God. His strength flows from obedience and his legacy flows from faithfulness. In a world that celebrates rebellion, bravado, and self-rule, the man who fears the Lord stands apart. He is anchored. He is unshakable. He is dangerous to darkness. The fear of the Lord is the foundation of real manhood. Men who lack the fear of God often collapse under pressure. Men who fear God stand firm when others fold.

God also wants a man of truth and integrity. Strength without integrity is dangerous, but integrity without compromise is powerful. In a world where deception is tolerated and half-truths are celebrated; God still searches for men whose yes is yes and whose no is no. A man of truth lives the same in private as he does in public. He does not wear one face for the crowd and another for the quiet moments of life. God desires men whose character does not shift with convenience, pressure, or popularity. Integrity means being whole and undivided. It's when you walk in alignment between what you believe, what you speak, and how you live. Truth is not simply something a man knows; it is something he walks in. God's truth shapes a man's decisions, disciplines his words, and governs his actions. A man of integrity refuses shortcuts, even when no one is watching. He understands that God sees the heart, weighs the motives, and honors faithfulness over an outward show, over those who shine the brightest.

Integrity is the foundation of trust. God entrusts responsibility, influence, and leadership to men who can be trusted with truth. When a man chooses honesty over advantage, righteousness over recognition, and obedience over approval, heaven takes notice. God builds His kingdom through men who will stand firm even when truth is costly. A man of truth does not bend his convictions to fit the moment. He stands anchored in God's Word, knowing that truth is not defined by culture but by the unchanging nature of God Himself. When he falls, he does not hide - he repents. When he is corrected, he does not resist - he grows. Integrity is not perfection; it is humility paired with obedience. God wants men whose lives preach louder than their words, men whose integrity becomes a shelter for their families, a witness to the world, and a stronghold against compromise. Such men leave a legacy not built on reputation, but on righteousness. He is always honored by God and that honor lasts forever.

God wants a man who takes responsibility. He is not looking for a man who makes excuses - He is looking for a man who owns his actions, a man who stands accountable, a man who bears the burden, and a man who answers the call. From the beginning, responsibility was part of man's design. When God placed Adam in the garden, He didn't give him comfort - He gave him a job to lead, to protect, to cultivate, and to steward. Before there was a wife, before there was a fall, before there was conflict - there was responsibility. Man was created to carry weight, not run from it. A responsible man does not blame others for his failures. He doesn't blame his past, his upbringing, the economy, or the culture. He looks in the mirror and says, "This is my assignment, and I will answer for it." God honors the man who owns his decisions - both good and bad. Responsibility is the bridge between potential and purpose. Many men have talent, strength, and opportunity but without responsibility, those gifts rot.

God does not promote men who refuse accountability. He promotes men who stand up and say, "If this is broken, I will fix it. If there is a need, I will supply what is missing." Throughout Scripture, God consistently chose men who accepted responsibility. David owned his sin and repented. Nehemiah took responsibility for a broken wall he did not destroy. Joseph took responsibility in prison as faithfully as in the palace. Jesus took responsibility for a world He did not corrupt. Real masculinity is not dominance - it is ownership. A responsible man leads his home spiritually. He guards his heart morally. He works diligently. He keeps his word. He stands in the gap when others step back. He understands that authority always follows responsibility and never the other way around. God is not impressed by loud men, tough talk, or empty bravado. He is moved by men who quietly shoulder the load and say, "Lord, You can trust me." God is still calling for men who will take responsibility. Man up and be that man.

It should come as no surprise that God also wants a man of courage, a man with holy boldness. A man of God is not defined by silence, fear, or compromise but by a strength that does not come from ego, anger, or intimidation, but from an unshakable confidence in God. In the world there is no shortage of loud men, but it is desperately short of bold righteous men. Courage is not the absence of fear; it is obedience in the presence of fear. Holy boldness is the willingness to stand when it would be easier to sit, to speak when it would be safer to remain silent, and to obey God when compromise would be more convenient. Scripture repeatedly shows that God moves through men who refuse to shrink back. He said to Joshua, "Have I not commanded you? Be strong and courageous. Do not be afraid; do not be discouraged, for the Lord your God will be with you wherever you go" (Joshua 1:9). This command was not given to a king seated on a throne - it was given to a man about to go forward into battle.

The man God wants does not shrink back when obedience is costly. He does not remain silent when truth must be spoken. Courage shows up when standing for righteousness invites criticism, doing the right thing feels lonely. Faith requires risk and obedience demands sacrifice. This generation does not need softer men. It needs strong, courageous, God-fearing men - men who pray boldly, love fiercely, lead faithfully, and stand unashamed for righteousness. Make the decision today to be a man of courage. A man of God does not wait to feel brave. He chooses obedience. David ran toward Goliath while trained soldiers froze in fear. Gideon tore down idols before he ever led an army. Peter preached boldly only days after denying

Jesus. In each case, courage followed obedience - not comfort. Courage is not optional for a man of God. It is part of his calling. You've got to man up because when one man walks in courage and holy boldness, heaven moves and others find the strength to stand with him.

The man God wants walks in humility. He knows who he is, but he also knows who God is. He does not exalt himself, demand recognition, or insist on his own way. A humble man listens before speaking, learns from correction, serves without needing applause, and gives God credit for his success. A humble man recognizes that everything he has comes from God, and therefore he walks with gratitude, teachability, and obedience. God also wants you to be a man of prayer. The man God wants understands that strength does not come from self-reliance but from dependence on God. Prayer is where battles are won before they are ever seen. A praying man seeks God's wisdom before making decisions, draws strength in times of weakness, intercedes for his family, church, and community, and aligns his will with God's will. Men who do not pray often struggle in silence. Men who pray walk with confidence - not because they know everything, but because they trust the One who does.

God is not merely interested in what a man does - He is deeply invested in who a man becomes. True manhood is not defined by strength alone, success alone, or even good intentions. It is defined by commitment so be a man who commits his heart, his ways, and his future fully to God. This is not a passive surrender; it is an active decision to place every part of life under

God's authority. When a man commits his heart, he aligns his desires with God's desires. His affections change. What once ruled him no longer controls him. His heart becomes soft toward God and strong toward righteousness. When a man commits his ways to God, his daily walk is transformed. His decisions, habits, and responses begin to reflect God's wisdom rather than impulse. Integrity replaces compromise. Faith replaces fear. Discipline replaces excuses. He no longer asks, "What do I want?" but "What honors God? What does He want?" This is where obedience becomes power, and consistency becomes influence.

When a man commits his future to God, he surrenders control of life's outcomes. He stops trying to force doors open and begins trusting God to lead him where he needs to go. He understands that God sees what he cannot see, knows what he does not know, and prepares what he cannot imagine. This kind of trust produces peace, courage, and unwavering confidence even in uncertain seasons. When a man fully commits himself to God, God fully commits Himself to that man. God begins to work through him in powerful ways. His words carry weight. His example carries authority. His presence brings stability. Through him, God changes lives, families, and generations. Families are strengthened because of him. Children are raised with vision because of him. Generations are impacted because one man decided to stand in obedience and faith. God uses him as a vessel to bring healing where there was brokenness, order where there was chaos, and hope where there was despair.

Becoming the man God wants is not about perfection - it is about surrender. When a man commits his heart, his ways, and his future into God's hands, something powerful begins to happen. God doesn't merely improve a man; He transforms him. A man who gives his heart to God learns to live from the inside out. His decisions are no longer driven by impulse, pride, or fear, but by conviction and obedience. He seeks God not only in moments of crisis, but in daily choices - in how he speaks, how he loves, how he works, and how he leads. Quiet faithfulness becomes his strength. When a man commits his ways to the Lord, his path begins to straighten. God shapes his character through responsibility, humility, and perseverance. Trials no longer exist to break him, but to refine him. Pressure reveals purpose and resistance builds resolve. This kind of man becomes a vessel of honor through whom God can shift the direction of a household, influence a community, and bless generations yet unborn.

God is not looking for perfect men. He is looking for available men - men who will say, "Lord, here I am. Shape me. Use me. Lead me." When a man fully commits his heart, his ways, and his future to God, he becomes the man God wants and through him, God does what only God can do. The man God wants is not born - he is formed on the potter's wheel. He is shaped through obedience, refined through trials, and strengthened through faith. This calling is not reserved for a select few; it is extended to every man willing to surrender his life to God. God is not asking you to be perfect. He is asking you to be willing to obey, willing to grow, willing to stand, willing to repent, and willing to trust. The world may applaud strength without character, but God honors character with strength. When a man commits his heart, his ways, and his future to God, he becomes the man God wants and through him the world becomes a better place. This is the man God wants. And this is the man God is calling you to become.

SUMMARY

This book has made one truth unmistakably clear: passivity is a choice - and so is strength. No man drifts into boldness by accident, and no man becomes strong and mighty by remaining on the sidelines of his own life. To "man up" is not about hype or momentary resolve; it is about a decisive shift in how you think, speak, and live every single day.

Throughout these pages, you have been challenged to confront the subtle habits of retreat - silence when you should speak, hesitation when you should act, comfort when you should press forward. Passivity rarely announces itself loudly. It disguises itself as patience, humility, or caution, but its fruit is always the same: lost ground, diminished influence, and unfulfilled purpose. Strength, on the other hand, requires intention. It demands courage, discipline, and a willingness to carry responsibility without excuse.

"Man Up!" has shown that boldness is not recklessness, confidence is not arrogance, and strength is not cruelty. True manhood is steady under pressure, firm in conviction, and unwavering in responsibility. A strong man does not wait to be pushed - he steps forward because he understands what is at stake. A mighty man does not shrink when opposition arises - he stands, adapts, and overcomes.

This journey has not been about becoming someone else. It has been about reclaiming who you were created to be. The strength you need is not something you must invent - it is something you must awaken. When you reject passivity, you take ownership of your life. When you embrace responsibility, you step into authority. When you choose courage over comfort, you begin to live with purpose.

Now the question is no longer whether you understand these truths but whether you will live them. Knowledge without action changes nothing. Conviction without commitment fades quickly. This closing is not an ending; it is a line in the sand. What you do next will determine the man you become and the legacy you leave behind.

The world does not need more men who are informed but inactive. It needs men who are willing to stand, lead, protect, build, and persevere. Men who refuse to retreat when things get difficult. Men who choose strength when weakness would be easier. Men who understand that boldness is not optional when responsibility is theirs to carry.

As you turn the final page, make the decision to move forward differently. Speak with confidence. Act with courage. Lead with strength. Stand firm when pressure comes. Reject passivity in every form and embrace the call to live strong and mighty.

This is not the end of the message. This is the beginning of the mandate. It's time now more than ever to Man Up!

www.ingramcontent.com/pod-product-compliance
Lightning Source LLC
Chambersburg PA
CBHW070908130626
46555CB00001B/56